Alan Cumming

Memoir

A Father's Son, A Journey Of Discovery

Mark Whittington

TABLE OF CONTENTS

CHAPTER 1
THE STORM IN HIS EYES

CHAPTER 2
LESSONS IN FEAR

CHAPTER 3
UNEXPECTED

CHAPTER 4
A FATHER'S SHADOW

CHAPTER 5
THE CALL THAT NEVER CAME

CHAPTER 6
CONVERSATIONS IN THE SNOW

CHAPTER 7
SILENT ECHOES

CHAPTER 8
THE PAST IN PIECES

CHAPTER 9
WOUNDS THAT TIME FORGOT

CHAPTER 10
BOX

CHAPTER 11
IN THE WAKE OF SILENCE

CHAPTER 12
GRANDFATHER'S LEGACY

CHAPTER 13
JOURNEY ACROSS GENERATIONS

CHAPTER 14
INHERITANCE OF TRUTH

CHAPTER 15
REFLECTIONS IN THE COBWEBS

CHAPTER 1
THE STORM IN HIS EYES

My father had barely glanced at me across the kitchen table while speaking, but I could sense the impending storm in his eyes.

"You need a haircut, boy!"

I attempted to speak, but the fear that had enveloped me made it difficult to swallow, and all that came out was a small gasping sound that pained my throat much more. And I knew that speaking would only make matters worse, increase his hatred for me, and cause him to pounce sooner. Waiting was the worst part. I never knew when it would arrive, and I know that was his favourite part.

As usual, we ate our evening meal in near silence until my father spoke. Until recently, my older brother, Tom, would have been seated where I am now, helping to divert the stare of imminent fury that was now fixed on me. But Tom has a job now. He always departed in a shirt and tie, which irritated our father. Tom was no longer under his control. Tom had escaped. I hadn't been as lucky yet.

My mother attempted to intercede. "I'll take him to the barber's on Saturday morning, Ali," she told me.

"He will work on Saturday. He's not going to get away with slouching off at work again. Do you hear me? There is too much of that going on in this house.

"Yes," I answered.

But now I realised it was a hopeless cause. It wasn't just a haircut; it was now my physical limitations as a labourer, my failure to complete the jobs he assigned me every weekend and many evenings, tasks I couldn't do because I was twelve, but largely because he wanted me to fail so he could hit me.

You see, I understand my father. I had learned from a young age to understand the tone of every word he said, his body language, and the energy he exuded in the room. It has not been easy as an adult to know that dealing with my father's aggression marked the beginning of my acting education.

"I can get one tomorrow at school lunchtime." My voice drifted off in a way I knew sounded too begging and weak, but I couldn't help myself.

"Yes, do that, pet," my mother responded, kindly.

I could detect optimism in her tone, and I admired her for it. But I realised it was false optimism and denial. This was bound to end horribly, and there was no way to avoid it.

Every night, getting off the school bus and strolling through the estate gates, across my father's sawmill yard, and into our house felt like a lottery. Will he be home yet? What would his mood be? I felt a little safer as soon as I walked into the house, changed out of my school uniform, and started doing my chores—bringing wood and coal in for the stove, starting the fire, setting the table, warming the dishes, and putting the potatoes to boil. You see, by then I was on his domain, under his direction, working for him, and this appeared to calm my father, as if my complete obedience was vital for his well-being. Of course, I was never fully safe, but those activities were so entrenched in me, and I felt confident that even if he did inspect them, I would pass muster, allowing me to breathe a bit better until we went down to eat.

My father was the head forester at Panmure Estate, located near Carnoustie on Scotland's east coast. The estate was immense, with fifty farms and thousands of acres of woodland spread across twenty-one square miles. We resided on the estate's "premises," which were the grounds of Panmure House, albeit the huge house had long since disappeared by the time we moved in. In 1955, as one of several austerity measures imposed on the landed nobility, its treasures were deconstructed and subsequently demolished with explosives. All that remained were the stables, where I'd report on chilly Saturday mornings during hunting season, banging my wellies together to keep my toes warm, to work as a beater, hitting trees with a stick in a line of other country boys, scaring the birds into the air so that drunk rich men could shoot at them.

The edifice that had formerly served as the house's chapel remained attached to the stables. It was now utilised for the annual estate Christmas party, as well as occasional dances or card game evenings for employees. We lived in Nursery House, so named because it overlooked a tree nursery where seedlings were hatched and nourished to replace the trees that were regularly chopped and returned to the sawmill that sat in the yard behind us. My father was in charge of the entire process, from the seeds to the cut lumber and everything in between, as well as the overall maintenance of the property.

It was all very feudal and reminiscent of Downton Abbey, minus the abbey and set fifty years later. I answered the door to a man who called my father "The Maister." There were gamekeepers, great gates, sweeping drives, and follies, but no lord of the manor because the property was owned by a family shipping company, a racehorse owner's charitable trust, and finally a large insurance company during the period we lived there.

I didn't realise it at the time, but I was living through the end of an age of magnificent Scottish estates, which, like Panmure, have now mostly been disassembled and sold off. Looking back, it was a lovely place to grow up, but at the time, all I wanted to do was escape as far away as possible.

I noticed my father's van sitting by the tractor shed as I walked past. So he was home. But he might not have been in the house; he could have been talking to one of his men in the sawmill, warehouse, or shed. It was the time of day when they returned from the woods and cleaned their tools before heading home. I couldn't see my father, and I didn't want to be seen looking for him in case he observed me and realised that my anxiety was leading my search. That would be his opening. Perhaps someone in the yard, such as a farmer or his boss, the estate factor (or manager), would come to visit him and enable me to pass without scrutiny.

I turned the corner onto our driveway at the bottom of the sawmill yard and noticed a light on in his office. My heart fell. He was seated at his desk by the window and looked up when he noticed me. I immediately straightened up, trying to recall everything he had recently informed me was wrong about me. I hoped my hair was combed the way he liked it, my school bag was hanging at the proper angle, and my shoes were shiny enough. It probably only took ten seconds for me to reach the front door and out of his sight, but in that brief moment, a slew of worries about my defects and failings raced through my head.

He was on the phone, thank goodness. He didn't leave his office until my mother returned home from work, and having her around always made me feel better. She finished brewing our tea as we talked. Then we heard him approaching the house, and we were silent. We both knew it wasn't a good idea to speak until we'd appraised him, and it didn't seem like a good idea to speak tonight.

My father sat in his chair at the kitchen table, and my mother promptly placed his plate of food in front of him. This is how it has always worked. Any departure, much alone a complaint about the cuisine, might set him off. Without recognizing her or me, he took his cutlery and began eating. He ate like an animal, not because he was dirty or loud, but because he ripped into his food with strength, stealth, and efficiency. It was horrible to witness.

My father remained silent for a while after my mother talked, and I hoped that going to the barbershop during school lunch break the next day would satisfy him. All I could think of was finishing this lunch and heading upstairs to complete my homework, or better yet, hiding in the woods with my dog. But my mouth was dry, and there was a ball of terror stuck in the top of my chest, making it difficult to swallow. I needed to get some water or else I'd choke or cry. I got up from the table and went to the sink. I grabbed up a glass from the draining board and began filling it.

"What the hell do you think you're doing?" he asked, not quite shouting but yet too loud, as if he'd been waiting to say it, eager to make the next move, and now it was time.

"Eh? "Have you heard me?"

"I need to drink some water," I exclaimed.

"Put that glass down!" Now he was shouting.

My mother spoke calmly, "Ali, leave him."

My father stood from his chair, and everything turned red. As dad began shouting at me, he grabbed me by the scruff of the neck and dragged me across the kitchen, living room, hallway, out through the porch and front door, and across the yard to the shed where we stored our bikes. He threw me on top of a workbench. He was baying now, rather than shouting. You couldn't hear what he was saying, but I knew it was about my hair, drinking water, and how fucking useless, insolent, and sad I was, but it wasn't cohesive. It was pure savage hatred, and it was aimed at me.

There was only one bare lightbulb dangling from the shed ceiling. I recall glancing up at it while he rummaged through a drawer behind me. Soon, his hand forced my head forward, the other holding a rusted pair of clippers that he had used on the sheep in the field in front of our house. They were blunt, unclean, and wounded my skin, but my father used them to shave my head while holding me down like an animal.

I was hysterical now, just like he was, but I knew he enjoyed hearing me cry, and it would be over faster if I was silent and limp. But that was so difficult. I was in pain and shock, and I hadn't taken a drop of water yet. I felt like I was about to pass out while attempting to catch my breath. All I could do was wait till the end. It eventually ended. He pushed my head one way and then the other to evaluate his work before throwing the clippers back into the drawer.

"Get your haircut appropriately! "Do you hear me?" he asked, his fury subsiding as he came down, exhausted.

"Yes," I tried not to whimper.

He smacked me across the back of my skull and vanished. The shed door pounded, forcing me to climb down from the bench. I made certain to clean up the mess. I grabbed the clumps of my hair that had fallen to the floor and carried them to the garbage bin outside. I returned to the shed to ensure that everything was back to normal before turning off the lone lightbulb and returning to the home. When I heard my father's van go up the sawmill yard, I paused for a second, filled with amazement and relief that he was gone.

In the restroom, I drank water from the tap. As I sipped, bits of hair dropped into the sink, and I felt blood dripping on my neck. Finally, I stood up and looked at my reflection.

I resembled a concentration camp inmate, and I wanted to die. At that moment, I wanted to die. My mother attempted to straighten up the mess with scissors to make it appear less uneven, but there were spots that had no hair left at all and could not be hidden. I'd have to go to school looking like this. I cried throughout the night. My eyes were so red and puffy the next morning that they nearly closed, but I was relieved since they distracted from my head. I informed my professors that I reached up to a high shelf and knocked over a jar of creosote (a tar-based wood preservative), getting some in my eyes. When queried about my hair, I explained that I had attempted to cut it myself.

I've tried more haircuts than most men my age have had hot dinners.

It doesn't take a genius to figure out that part of the reason I've loved changing the colour, length, and appearance of my follicles over the years has to do with reclaiming the power my father took away from me in this (and other) areas as a youngster. My hair has been blond on multiple occasions; it has been short and spiky, long and floppy, smooth, scruffy, and everything in between. I've even faced the clipper demons and shaved my own head several times.

However, it took some time to get here. In my late teens, there were multiple occasions when I was in a hair salon and suddenly felt queasy, and twice I vomited, not recognizing until many years (and a lot of therapy) later that my body was showing physically what I couldn't yet handle emotionally. I obviously had some extremely hidden and traumatic memories. However, once I had left home and was free of my father's grip, I began to use my hair as a sign of my own freedom. One time in drama school, in a particularly symbolic gesture of self-assertion, I accepted to have my youthful locks dyed purple by an overzealous hairdressing student and returned to my parents' house for the weekend with my head held high, and nothing, not a word, was uttered. (I did wear a purple sweater to divert all of the focus, but it was still ballsy, don't you think?!)

I think what I'm saying is... I am OK. I outlived my father. My mother, brother, and I all did it, both literally and figuratively.

However, like with all difficult tasks, it was a process.

CHAPTER 2
LESSONS IN FEAR

*M*emory is quite subjective. We all recall in a visceral, emotional way, so even if we agree on the facts—what was said, where, and when—what we take away and store from a moment, and how we feel about it, might differ dramatically.

I truly wanted to illustrate that not everything in my family was negative. I tried so hard to remember wonderful times we had together, when we had fun and laughed. In the spirit of balance, I also wanted to be able to express certain occasions of kindness and tenderness involving all of us. But I simply couldn't.

I chatted with my brother about it. He drew a blank, too.

We remember good times with our mother. Safe and calm times. But as a family? Honestly, there isn't a single memory from our childhood that isn't tinged with dread, embarrassment, or sorrow. That is not to suggest that moments of enjoyment did not exist; rather, they have been overshadowed by the overwhelming emotions that colour all of our childhood memories.

I recall we were all at a Chinese restaurant in a nearby town. We rarely ate out, so when we did, it was a special occasion. But there is something irritating about my memories of that area, something that pricks at my heart whenever I think about it. I know that at least once in the few occasions we went there as a family, I was slapped for some defect my father saw, and I had to hide my tears and embarrassment from the other diners. We undoubtedly had some dinners there that were devoid of his mood swings, his tongue, and the back of his hand, but they did not jump out at me.

I recall playing horsey with my father in the living room of Panmure when I was about four or five years old. I envision dad placing me on the foot of his crossed leg while watching TV and bouncing me up and down to my squeals of joy. I recall feeling genuinely joyful on those occasions. But as soon as that memory becomes too ingrained in my mind, another, darker one pushes it aside.

I see a cold, winter afternoon in the sawmill yard. I am riding the red bike I received for Christmas, and my father has decided that today is the day I shall ride it without training wheels. To this day, I have never attempted to ride without them. There is ice and snow on the ground, and I witness my father remove the training wheels and push me down the driveway too quickly. Every time he does this, I panic and fall off, and he quickly becomes irritated with my failure, pulling my trousers down and slapping me hard on my bare bum. It is so cold that I have no sensation in my toes and hardly in my fingers; it is painful for me to sit down on the seat; I am afraid and crying; and yet, my father believes I will be able to accomplish what he has determined I must do. Each time I fall, despite my pleadings and vows that I will practise and be able to ride without the training wheels soon, I am bent over his knee, feeling a blast of icy air around my genitals, and then receiving harsh, excruciating smacks to my bottom.

I can't recall how it finished. What I do remember is my mother washing me and preparing me for bed in front of the living room fire later that night, and her gasping when she noticed the ring of blue, black, and purple bruises that had emerged. My father came in to say goodbye before heading out for the night, and my mother chastised him for his work.

"He's all right," he said, looking in the mirror and brushing a comb through his hair.

"You've gone too far, Ali," my mother said as he disappeared out the door.

Aside from family visits, we spent most of our vacations together at caravan (or RV) parks in seaside towns throughout Scotland. I remember when I was around seven, we travelled to Dunbar on the southeast coast, and I got to ride the go-carts.

Now came what I recall as a period of unending darkness, silence, and fear. Being around him felt like navigating a minefield. We couldn't relax. We were never safe. He started going out every night. I recall sitting in the living room with my mother and hearing him getting dressed upstairs. The door eventually opened, and his head appeared.

"That puts me away!"

But he'd be gone before the words were out of his mouth, his eyes not even meeting ours. It was as if he was saying good night to a pet, and he soon stopped saying it completely.

I had no idea what had happened, but I assumed it was my fault. He was constantly telling me how much of a disappointment I was, both in my appearance—my hair, of course, but also my posture, weight, nose, and moles—and in my inability to perform even the most basic of tasks, despite the fact that his lack of detail in explaining what he wanted me to do or the physical enormity of what was required guaranteed my failure. He once requested that I drive a tractor, despite the fact that I had never done so before and had received no tutoring on how to do so from him or anybody else. I tried to reason with him. He frequently assigned me massive jobs that would keep me busy until dusk or later, but this was another level. Now he was asking me to imperil my life by handling big machinery, and I got terrified. My father began shouting at me, and I knew I had to comply with his demands. I climbed up onto the upper seat. My feet did not even reach the pedals. Of course, I messed it up, and the tractor lurched into a hedge before stalling. I was hit, and perhaps for the first time, the violence eased me since it signalled the end of an exceedingly unpleasant and stressful situation.

One night, as he peeked his head around the door and lobbed his normal "That's me away," I asked him where he was headed."

My mother looked up from her crocheting, and my father halted in his tracks. I asked with no malice. I was honestly fascinated. But no one ever questioned my father, and I could tell I was on solid ground.

"Do you want to come with me?"My father answered defensively.

"So, where are you going?"I asked again.

"You tell me if you want to come and I'll tell you where I'm going."

I thought about this for a bit. I knew my father was heading out. He was dressed up, smelled like Old Spice, and had Brylcreemed hair. If he went to the pub, I wouldn't be let in and would be forced to spend the evening in his vehicle, which I didn't want. But I had a feeling there was more to it than that, and I believe my parents knew.

My mother said nothing.

"So, will you come or not?"After a few moments, my father announced that he had won.

"No," I answered humbly.

I'm not sure how I found out, whether it was through school gossip or something I overheard at home, but I quickly realised that my father's conduct had changed because he was seeing another lady, and that Tom and I were a continuous reminder of the life that had ensnared him.

Soon after, on a bright Sunday afternoon, we all headed to Carnoustie Beach. As I previously stated, we rarely did anything together, especially anything as carefree and fun as a trip to the beach. Summers are brief in Scotland, so we take advantage of even the smallest glimmer of sun, and that day was no exception. Every time the sun appeared from behind the clouds, we dashed along the sand into the icy North Sea, dipping under the waves for a few moments before sprinting back up the beach to the shade of our striped windbreak, an essential component of any Scottish beach adventure.

I'm standing on the platform of a massive marquee that hosts the Cinema Against AIDS Gala in the gardens of the Hôtel du Cap, just outside Cannes. I'm looking out at a sea of wealthy, tanned, chatty French folks, all sipping champagne and conversing with one another, ignoring me and smoking, smoking, smoking.

I should point out that I'm not alone on stage. I'm surrounded by Patti Smith and Marion Cotillard, and we're just standing there doing nothing. Luckily, no one in the audience is paying any attention to us, and we feel imprisoned in celebrity aspic.

Suddenly, the trance is shattered by a sheepish voice that turns out to be my own, speaking into the microphone, "Um, sorry about this delay, ladies and gentlemen, we're, eh, just waiting for Mary J. Blige to return to the stage so we can auction off a duet with her and Patti."

Patti Smith's head snapped round towards me so quickly that I felt a draft. Panic made her eyes appear even more alien than I remembered when she passed me on her way to the stage earlier in the evening. Right now, she resembled one of the girls in The Crucible, fresh from a horrible vision.

You may not be aware, but Patti Smith is prone to spitting. I first met her at a gathering in a New York City clothes store a few years ago. She sang a couple songs as cute young black folks meandered around, offering canapés and champagne to less cute older black individuals. It wasn't particularly rock and roll, but Patti changed that. In between two of her songs, she spat. Not a "Oops, I've got a little something stuck on my tongue" spit, but a huge, throat-curdling gob of spit. A loogie, as the Americans say. She spat on the carpet. Multiple times.

No one in the store mentioned Patti's spitting, least of all me, when I was taken to meet her after the performance. As we were introduced, I noticed Patti weighing me up warily with her Dickensian eyes.

Can you envision Patti Smith emerging from the shadows in a black suit, rambling on about Inspector Linley or some wrongdoing on the Orient Express, and concluding each introduction with a thunderous gob into a specially built PBS spittoon? I can. It would be far more fascinating than that dude in a suit with the amusing accent they have now.

Meanwhile, Marion had walked to the side of the stage, crying, "Do something! Do something!"

I admired her Gallic sense of injustice, but I knew her protests would be in vain. These types of events, while appearing fashionable and sophisticated on the outside, are frequently staged with the delicacy of a kindergarten nativity play, and the teachers are all lapsed Narcotics Anonymous members.

Patti and I were both numb as we stood centre stage. She was probably going through a list of tunes she and Mary J. Blige would know, which couldn't have taken long.

My first Cannes appearance was in 1992, when my debut feature picture, Prague, opened. Looking back, it was all a blur of excitement. My only previous film festival experience was in Scotland, where a film I had created in my final term of theatre school, Gillies McKinnon's Passing Glory, premiered at the Edinburgh Film Festival in 1986. I remember that event vividly because it was the first time I had ever seen myself on a large screen, and I was startled by how my nose appeared at least fifteen seconds before the rest of my face. A less confident man might have avoided the camera for good.

But I persevered, and now I'm cruising the Croisette and monter l'escalier of the Palais des Congrès, rather than strolling up the Lothian Road and going into the Edinburgh Film House. That week, I discovered for the first time that glamour had a fragrance. However, I was reminded that the industry I worked in was show business.

Film festivals are essentially business gatherings, you see. It could be photocopiers or shower curtains; Cannes, however, is about movies. And I believe that any business convention, even one as glamorous as the Cannes Film Festival, can only be interesting for so long because too many people are talking about the same thing: their jobs or products—as photocopiers, shower curtains, and films are now referred to. Don't get me wrong, I enjoy my job and talking about movies, but if that's all there is to talk about for days on end, I become bored.

That night, in my lovely suite at the Hôtel du Cap, which looked out onto the wonderful terrace that sloped down to the shimmering Mediterranean, where paparazzi dinghies bobbed in the wake, I had some weird dreams. I imagined I was back onstage in the tent, and Harvey was auctioning off a kiss with me for $30,000, and no one was buying! The fact that Ryan Gosling had experienced this earlier that evening simply added to the nightmare.

"No, Harvey," I repeatedly said. "Become more realistic. Begin at one hundred pounds!"

I also had a dream about my mother, who was feverishly knitting numerous pairs of socks to give as Christmas gifts to all of her new Asian acquaintances.

Yes, I will run it by you again. The next day, I was scheduled to fly to London to prepare for the production of an episode of the BBC television show Who Do You Think You Are?, a very popular program in which celebrities have their ancestors researched, and studious, balding guys in tweed coats with leather patches on the elbows assist the stars in poring over ancient parchments containing family secrets. But not for long, as a previously unknown secret is disclosed, and the celebrity screams.

I was asked at the end of the previous year whether I would be interested in participating in the show, and I quickly answered yes. Then followed the unsettling several months when the production firm went off and performed some preliminary research to determine whether my past was worthy of a full hour-long investigation. In other words, they needed to decide if my forebears were intriguing enough. As an actor, I've grown accustomed to waiting for others to cast judgement on me—audiences, critics, awards juries, fashion police—on such a regular basis that it's almost no longer shocking. But this was different. This time, the judgement wasn't about me, but it did reflect on me.

And I was extremely eager to do this show because it would allow me to finally solve a riddle in my mother's side of the family, one whose received explanation I had never fully accepted and knew would be settled by the program once and for all. As a result, I had a dream about my mother making socks for all of the new family members I expected to find.

Well, there were two family mysteries. The other one featured my father's family, the Cumming clan of Cawdor. Yes, that Cawdor, "Glamis thou art, and Cawdor; and shalt be what thou art promised" and so on. Cawdor is a little village surrounded by forest and farming in northern Scotland, and Shakespeare set Macbeth there without having to explore the fact that the real Macbeths never visited the area because they died three hundred years before Cawdor Castle was completed. (This lack of historical detail lends credence to my theory that if Shakespeare were living today, he would write for television, but in a more sophisticated setting.)

For as long as anyone could remember, my father's family had worked on the Cawdor estate farm. Return to the 1980s. Cawdor's lairds, like many privately owned Scottish castles, were feeling the pinch and decided to open their residence to the public, resulting in a flood of postcards of this photograph sent to me by various friends who had seen the castle. ..Do you think there was a dalliance down stairs at any point? Perhaps the helper provided a bit extra? Hello?!

I am struck by the similarities between this figure, John Campbell, the First Lord of Cawdor (painted by Sir Joshua Reynolds in 1778 and still hanging in the castle's drawing room today), and myself. I have a postcard of it in my study, and numerous acquaintances have mistaken it for a still from a period film I've made.

My imagination is quite vivid and knows no limitations at the best of times, but it went into overdrive tonight, as I dreamed about future episodes of Who Do You Think You Are? showing that I was, in fact, the true Earl of Cawdor, followed by a special follow-up episode explaining the hardships of switching from my jet-setting Hollywood existence to that of a Scottish laird dealing with cranky American tourists and wet banquet halls.

Of course, I understood that aside from going to Cawdor and yanking a chunk of hair off the current earl's head for a DNA test, which was not within the purview of the pretty scholarly techniques of Who Do You Think You Are?—I would have no method of demonstrating the authenticity of my prospective minor aristocratic claim. If some randy laird long ago got a chambermaid up the duff, injecting the Cumming bloodline with bluish blood, he would hardly rush to the village clerk to have it recorded in the chronicles for TV researchers to discover centuries later, would he?

No, the true mystery, which I was relieved to find that the show would focus on, concerns my maternal grandpa, Thomas Darling.

Although my mother, Mary, retained the surname Cumming following her divorce from my father, she is known to me, my brother Tom, and all of our friends by her maiden name, Mary Darling. She is not Mary; she is Mary Darling. This is primarily due to the fact that her name matches her so well. She is very adorable.

I had chatted with her numerous times the week before I arrived in Cannes, and she was getting increasingly excited about the start of filming. The concert was going to be about her father, after all, a guy she hadn't seen since she was eight years old, though he hadn't died until she was thirteen, five years later, in 1951.

Tommy Darling was born in the north of England, in an area known as the Borders due to its proximity to Scotland, and he was orphaned at the age of two. He married my grandmother and had four children: Mary Darling and her three younger brothers, Tommy, Don, and the now-deceased Raymond. He was a decorated soldier during WWII. But after the war, Tommy Darling never returned home. He joined the Malayan police force, died in a shooting accident, and was buried in neighbouring Singapore.

But why had he not returned to his family? What exactly were the circumstances surrounding this "shooting accident"?

In the days leading up to the start of filming, my mind raced with thoughts about the different possibilities of Tommy Darling's narrative, as well as how a family can have so little awareness of a relative only one generation away. When little is known and little is spoken about, it is so easy for obvious inaccuracies to be obscured by speculation and supposition. I realised I had no idea who my grandfather was, and neither did my mother or brother. Mary Darling's mother, my dear Granny, died a few years ago, but I never recall her talking about him. She had remarried after his death, and when her second husband died, she had added to Tommy Darling's burden.

If Mary Darling was excited, I was astounded. I enjoy surprises, you see. I enjoyed the notion that the production personnel would not tell me where I would be going on this journey until the day it began, and that each day could mean a different country, perhaps a continent! I had only been told that the first week of the shoot would take place in Europe (very vague!) and that I would begin in London but would require my passport at some point. I felt like a small boy again, like I was going to burst with anticipation and suspense. Worse, the show was generally shot in two consecutive weeks, but due to my filming schedule, the second week and finish of the plot would not take place for another month. I had no idea how I was going to contain myself for four weeks! I did know, however, that in two days' time, on Saturday morning in London, I had an appointment with a doctor to get some required jabs for the second part of the shoot, and after a quick search on the Internet, I discovered that the countries these vaccinations were required for included Singapore, so hey ho, call me Sherlock, I was pretty sure I knew where I was going to end up.

CHAPTER 3
UNEXPECTED

*W*hen I was younger, an older boy named David bullied me on the school bus. David's father was the head joiner (carpenter) on the estate, whereas ours was the head forester. Tom, six years older than me and a year older than David, had graduated from secondary school by then, and we parted ways each morning. Tom went to Carnoustie and the posh new high school, whereas I went to Monikie and the modest Victorian stone elementary school with just six students in my class. The bus I travelled aboard appeared to be from WWII, and it was. It was a large, imposing dark blue military transport vehicle with two long benches facing one another across a broad expanse of floor. Of course, the layout required you to never glance away from anyone. Everyone was always aware of everything that was going on.

Every afternoon on the way home, and some mornings, I was kicked, pushed, and slapped off the seat, my ears twisted back and forth, my books flung around and trodden on, the straps of my schoolbag held so I couldn't get away, and all the while, through my cries of pain and fear, his taunts that I no longer had a big brother to protect me rang in my ears. Fortunately, the journey back to the estate gates was brief, and as soon as the vehicle halted, I jumped out and bolted down the drive, much to the enjoyment of my tormentor and his younger siblings.

David was a good enough lad, and I now see that his bullying of me that summer was only his attempt to build the new world order of the Monikie school bus. My brother had been the unquestioned leader until he reached high school, so by scaring me, David was not only establishing himself as alpha male, but also as the new Tom

Cumming. What better way to demonstrate your previous leader's powerlessness than to make his younger brother cry?

But then I got upset as hell and refused to tolerate it any longer. I told Tom. Not much was spoken. Just an emotional confession when he inquired whether everything was fine at school without him. I almost forgot about it until one night, when we were cycling home from Cub Scouts. David and his siblings were in a pack ahead of us. Tom asked David to wait and then told me to go home.

"What are you going to do?" I inquired, immediately alarmed.

"Alan, just go home." I'll be there in a little while."

I did as instructed, pedalling quickly through the estate gates and down the driveway, through the sawmill yard to our house, and into the bike shed. My heart was pounding, and my mind was racing with thoughts of what horrible pain or bloodshed might be happening on my behalf right now. My folks did not seem to notice my anxiousness. When I entered the living room, my mother looked up from her ironing and asked where Tom was, while my father focused on the television. Minutes later, Tom came, cool as a cucumber, and gave me a stony look that told me we would never talk about this again.

Five minutes later, the doorbell rang, and I dashed out to answer it, my pulse racing. I opened the door to discover David, weeping and clutching his already bruised eye, being held up by his enraged mother.

"Get your father!!" David's mother yelled.

My father ushered them inside. Suddenly, our living area transformed into a trial, with me serving as both the smoking gun and the perpetrator.

"Your son gave my son a black eye," David's mother exclaimed.

"Well, Tommy, is this true?" our father screamed, but I could tell he was secretly pleased.

"Yes, it is!" Tom remarked, drawing himself up and accepting his sins. "But David's been bullying Alan on the school bus for months now."

Everything ceased. David's youthful embarrassment was now exposed for all to see. I felt sorry for him, this tiny adolescent who had pushed me out of my seat, flung my books around, held me down, and struck me numerous times. He'd never made me feel as mortified as he did now.

I was abruptly awakened from my empathetic trance by the awareness that the grownups had stopped shouting and David had stopped weeping. In fact, the entire room had stopped and was now staring at me, waiting for me to bring the whole miserable situation to an end.

"Well, Alan," my father said. "Is this true?"

The room became quiet. I could feel my cheeks flaming and everyone's eyes staring deep, laser-like into mine.

"No," I replied humbly.

As much as I wanted to support Tom's tribal quid pro quo, I also felt sorry for David, who was snivelling away, the bruise around his eye getting worse by the second. It was simply too much to deal with, so I chose what I felt was the lesser of two evils. As soon as I denied that he was my tormentor, I fell into tears, and the adults recognized they were placing a nine-year-old under undue strain, especially since David made no protest of innocence. The Clarks went home, I was consoled, and the subject was never discussed again. In some way, we all agreed that justice had been served. Eye for an eye. Or perhaps a black eye for a series of bruises and stinging ears.

I shared this anecdote during my brother's wedding. (This is his third, incidentally. We Cumming lads enjoy weddings.) For me, it represents our relationship: Tom, the protective older brother, and me, in awe of his love and tendency to screw things up.

In no time at all, I was in my London flat, laughing with pals.

Aside from the mysterious visits I planned to go elsewhere, I was supposed to be based there for the first week of filming Who Do You Think You Are? My old friends Sue and Dom were waiting for me, and I was looking forward to catching up and laughing about the craziness of the night before in Cannes, each anecdote more delicious in its telling because it was no longer real life.

I could identify the palpable tension when the auctioneer told Jennifer Lopez that her clothing made her look like an ostrich, but I didn't have to see or feel it. There would be no concern that the star I was about to introduce would not be the same as the one who walked onstage. Actually, there would be no celebrities. Just me and my best friends.

Sue and I met many years ago at the Donmar Warehouse theatre in London. I was there playing Hamlet, followed by my role as the Emcee in Cabaret, which later moved to Broadway, and we had become closest friends ever since. Sue likes to tell people that she washed my undies when we first met, which she did because she was a stage dresser at the time. She was and continues to be breathtakingly beautiful. Quite literally. Her surname was originally Gore, but she legally changed it to Gorgeous after years of using it as an unofficial appellation. The actual document she had to sign to finish the name-changing process was funny, requiring her to solemnly pledge to renounce the name Gore and to be, from that day forward, Gorgeous. And she has been. When Sue married Dom, I and our other best friend, Andrew, were male bridesmaids, hiding our laughter as she walked down the aisle to Elvis singing "It's Now

Or Never."

As the wine poured and the laughter escalated, I felt at home, which was my favourite feeling. Then Sue's phone rang.

"Hi, Tom," she said. "Oh, he is here. He arrived almost an hour ago." I puzzled why my big brother would phone Sue rather than me to find out where I was. Sue handed me her phone, and I instantly realised something was wrong.

"How are you doing?" Tom inquired, a little nervous. Obviously, he did not mean to speak to me.

"I'm fine. How are you?" I responded cautiously.

"When am I going to see you then?"

"Do you remember tomorrow night? We're all having dinner," I added, alluding to the arrangement for him, his wife, Sonja, a group of my London friends, and me to meet at my favourite Chinese restaurant the following evening.

"I really need to talk to you, Alan."

There was a moment of stillness. I tried to understand what this meant.

"Well, why don't you come up a bit early tomorrow and have a drink with me at the flat before dinner," I replied.

"No, I need to talk to you sooner than that." Tom was trying to keep it together, but the cracks were starting to show.

"Tom, what's wrong?"

"I can't tell you on the phone, Alan."

"Is it your health?" My imagination quickly went to the worst-case possibilities. My brother is a rock. If he acted this way, it signalled there was something seriously wrong. "Has something happened between you and Sonja?"

"No, no."

I could hear Tom, even in the thick of whatever difficult situation he was going through, trying to reassure me. It was something he had always done for me.

"Is something wrong with Mum?" But I'd spoken to Mary Darling several times that week and had only heard her message. There was no way she could have kept something unpleasant from me.

I suddenly remembered what Mary Darling had said about the reporter. "Is it something to do with that Sunday Mail guy looking for Dad?"

"It's all come to a head, Alan," Tom replied. "I need to talk to you tonight."

It took Tom three hours to reach me. He lives in Southampton and had to catch a train, which meant three hours of my head racing and my heart pounding. Sue and Dom tried to divert me, but I could never get away from the worry. What could be making my brother so furious that he couldn't even say it to me on the phone? I was a disaster. My thoughts went to extremely dark places. The fact that the press was involved was extremely alarming.

If I had been able to think rationally at the time, I would have realised that there was nothing particularly shocking about my life that hadn't already been published or touched on, and I may have found comfort in the added benefit of becoming an open book. But I was having trouble finding solace anywhere. I started getting wheezy. I have asthma, and it flares up when I'm under a lot of stress. Sue, luckily, is a self-proclaimed hypochondriac and an expert on all homoeopathic cures, so I soon had a mouthful of tablets to distract me. But the niggling uneasiness lingered, and Tom had not arrived. He kept texting: "I'm on the train... I'm almost at Waterloo." I'm getting into a taxi.

I kept repeating our phone chat. Has my father died? Was it anything to do with my spouse, Grant? He was on his way home to New York City; what had happened to him? However, the reporter from the Sunday Mail remained at the heart of it all, as Tom had stated, and everything had come to a head. But what did this mean?

By the time he arrived, I felt like I had aged ten years. He entered the flat with a fairly normal appearance. No tears, no visible evidence of anguish. If anything, he appeared ashamed by all the commotion he must have caused by losing his phone. For a brief minute, my heart skipped a beat, and I wondered if this revelation, whatever it was, would be as ominous and harmful as I had anticipated. After a few awkward moments of small conversation, he stared at me.

"Shall we go upstairs?"

CHAPTER 4
A FATHER'S SHADOW

*E*very June, for a few days, something beautiful called the Angus Show takes place in Arbroath, a town about 10 miles from our home.

It was a conventional agricultural event, with sheep shearing, dog trials, highland cows, tractors, and tug-of-war, as well as trailers full of household products and souvenirs being peddled by men who enticed you to spend by shouting ever-decreasing prices over their tiny microphones. There were vendors offering all kinds of delicacies that, to a country kid like me, appeared extremely exotic. Items such as corn on the cob and donuts. But what I liked most about the Angus Show was the humanity, the seething throng that crowded Victoria Park. I enjoyed the feeling of being a part of a crowd, one among many. It made me feel safer.

Every year, as June approached, I'd see show posters on trees and telegraph poles all across the county. They were vibrant and full of promise, and I wished I could go. That was the point, though. I never knew if I'd be allowed to go. It would entail receiving a lift from my father, and because it was so impossible to predict his mood and readiness to keep his commitments, I soon stopped relying on him entirely and simply stopped asking him for a ride anyplace. Occasionally, a friend's father would agree to pick me up, but we lived in such a remote location that I rarely planned it. Furthermore, I knew my father would regard such an arrangement as a betrayal or act of weakness on my behalf. If I did, I'd make sure to be left off at the estate gates and not let the friends come anywhere near our house. This was originally intended to protect my family, but as I grew older, it became more about safeguarding my self-esteem than hiding my father's future actions. As I grew older, I became less anxious about people discovering what a monster Dad was. I was waiting for the day when I could leave home and get away from him.

Anyway, my brother and I biked almost everywhere. Even as children, we would cycle for miles up and down the hills and lanes of Angus. I truly believe that my muscular legs today are the result of daily hard leg workout during my formative years. We biked to Cubs and Scouts meetings, badminton at Monikie Hall, several miles there and back, and later, when we were older, we'd bike all the way to Carnoustie, at least a ten-mile round trip, beginning the journey by freewheeling down the enormous hill called the Marches just south of the estate gates, exhilarated by the rush of the wind as we sped and the rush to be free of our father's rule for a few hours. Cycling back up at the end of the night wasn't as exciting. But, as I mentioned, we both have calves to die for.

This particular summer, I was thirteen. As usual, I spent my whole summer break on the estate, brashing. Brushing entailed taking a saw attached to a long pole and cutting away all of the branches of a spruce tree as far up as you could reach and all the way down to the ground, allowing the tree to send its energy up to the higher branches and grow taller faster, as well as giving future foresters easier access when it came time to cut it down and send it to the sawmill.

Every morning at the crack of dawn, I set out with a few older boys, our saws awkwardly perched across the handlebars of our bikes, our packed lunches in bags thrown across our shoulders. We'd spend the day in some lonely part of the estate, brushing away, frequently abandoning our work to dash off in every direction to avoid wasp attacks on the nests we'd disturbed.

My father would come and check on our work at least once a day. When we heard his van approaching, we would instantly boost our efforts. Nobody, including me, wanted to get on his bad side. Often, one of us would be summoned back down our row to evaluate a subpar job on the tree. I dreaded walking across the forest floor, which was littered with freshly cut branches. He wouldn't hurt the other lads, only humiliate them. I tried not to give him any reason to strike me in front of them, but sometimes he did, and I had to endure the awkward silence as I returned to my saw, trying not to cry and wish the sting in my ear or cheek to go away.

In the past, the only times my father had taken me somewhere on his own initiative were bittersweet events. For, as much as I appreciated these occasional glimpses into a life that might have been—a supposedly loving father taking his son swimming or out to a café for a strawberry tart and a glass of pop—I knew he had made me an unwilling collaborator in his current affair. Years ago, I had a traumatic experience in the pool. She was waiting for us at the entryway. Neither my father nor her attempted to explain her look, and I knew not to question it. It was a woman I knew. I also knew her spouse. As I splashed around on my own in the shallow end, I could glimpse them farther up, smiling and nuzzling, she with her back against the pool wall, my father facing her, his arms outstretched, gripping the ledge on either side of her, right under a sign with a big "NO" at the top, followed by a list of the sorts of behaviour not tolerated in this establishment, including, to my horror, "HEAVY PETTING"—exactly what my father and this woman were engaging in right at that very moment.

Even as a small lad, I was astounded by my father's brazenness. There would have been others they knew in this pool who would have noticed them. They appeared to be unconcerned about the possibility that their activities would compromise or shame those individuals. I understood my father had no concern for anyone's feelings, let alone his wife's or his little son's, who at the time felt dragged down into a muck of lies and crime simply by being near them. My father then informed me that the woman would be joining us for a cup of tea and that I may have a strawberry tart, a seasonal delicacy so wonderful and uncommon that my brother and I would discuss it in hushed tones. Even while I appreciated it, I realised I was being bought.

But why did my father take me to these meetings, I've frequently wondered. He must have known my mother would inquire, and I would tell her that we had not been alone, and while my mother appeared to tolerate my father's rampant adultery, she refused to accept her children as accessories. As soon as we arrived home that day, they got into a heated argument.

My father was obviously using me in some way, but how? Was I invited over to remind this woman that, despite their clear and public connection, he was still a family man with obligations, and that their affair would always be limited to that? Or, worse, was I there as a decoy, presenting a softer, kinder side of my father to counterbalance the more brutish front he portrayed to the world? Perhaps he felt my presence made him and the woman appear more like a family, and so less illicit to those around us?

Back home, exhilarated from my father's uncommon attention and the sugar high of the soda and strawberry tart, I was brought crashing down when I saw my mother so angry. Soon after, my Saturday mornings were no longer mine, as I was assigned to work on the estate, peeling posts in the sawmill or weeding seedbeds in the nursery. It was backbreaking work, but I was relieved to avoid such compromising circumstances. Even strawberry tarts had lost their appeal.

Several years later, I could see that my father's desire to accompany me to the Angus Show was contingent on certain circumstances.

My mother looked up from her knitting and smiled warmly at me.

"No, pet. You go to the concert. I understand how much you want to.

Saturday arrived, and at the designated hour, we headed off in quiet. My earnings from the brawling were burning a hole in my wallet. I thought my father would allow me to spend some time on my own.

We had to park far away from the showground, but I enjoyed the stroll, the sounds and smells drawing closer as we approached. My father walked with resolve to the farm machinery section. There were stands with tractors and combine harvesters where you could get into their cabs and pretend to drive. I did not, of course. I was too old for that now, but I had done it as a child, and seeing other youngsters do it now made me pleased and nostalgic for those days. Then I noticed her standing casually by a stall selling brochures and key chains with tractor manufacturer logos. It was not the woman I expected, but she was not unfamiliar to me. We exchanged polite greetings, and they claimed it was a complete chance that we had run into each other in this boiling mass. Then my father took off, and she followed. I knew better than to loiter and hurriedly followed them.

Thus began an unusual dance. She and my father would be ahead of me, and then they were gone. Fearing the fury that would occur if I were lost, I began to worry and surveyed the area, hopping up and down to look over the heads in search of them. I weaved my way through the crowds to rejoin them, amazed at how quickly we had become separated and resolved to myself to be more diligent from now on. I overlooked stalls that would typically catch my sight. At one point, we came to an army recruitment trailer, and while I looked at the photographs of burly guys driving helicopters and tanks, I waited for my father to begin telling me about his time in the military. His National Service in the Royal Air Force was a source of great pride for dad, even though, as I grew older and began to ask more questions, I discovered he had just worked in the kitchens of his barracks and had never seen actual battle. Nonetheless, the order, discipline, and slavish adherence to rule had clearly left a strong impression on him. Of course, it entered my mind that Tom and I were now his soldiers.

However, the typical report of a fellow squaddie's incompetence did not appear that day. When I looked up, my father was gone. She was gone. They had both vanished into the masses, and I realised instantly that they had planned to do so, that they had been attempting to lose me for the past quarter of an hour. I had pursued them tenaciously, fearing my father's fury, unaware that he was plotting their escape all along. My father had purposefully abandoned me.

My instincts told me to try to find them, but knowing that they had purposefully tried to lose me calmed the panic in my gut. I reminded myself that I had done everything I could. Surely, my father would not have the audacity to punish me for this? I also began to formulate a plan. I reviewed my alternatives. It was bright, there were a lot of people around, and I had cash. But I knew that telling anyone about what had happened, even the public "I've lost my dad" version, would be unacceptable to him. Taking the bus to Muirdrum and then walking the final several miles to the estate would have been too much of a transgression, so it was also out of the question. My only option—which I assumed was the one my father desired and knew I would take—was to stay in the park, roam about until they returned, and take my chances. There was nothing left for me to do.

At the time, my brother Tom and his fiancée were busy putting together their "bottom drawer," a collection of domestic items for their future together that would accumulate during the course of their engagement. Each time they bought or received anything to add to it, it made me nervous since it indicated that the day Tom would leave me alone in our house was approaching. And I was jealous, for each pot or bedspread represented a future, another life, and a symbol of optimism that I could not yet comprehend.

But here, alone in a showground with people eager to sell me stuff and my wages simply ready to be spent, I did something that made my heart sing and undoubtedly had a deeper symbolic meaning. I purchased myself a dinner service!

I didn't mean to. After all, I was thirteen and probably wouldn't be hosting any dinner parties for a long time. But I needed to feel safe, to know that there was a future for me that did not include my father and a lady who was not my mother rushing around like school children trying to hide from me, darting off to the back of a carefully parked van on a peaceful side street. I needed to picture a house where I was not tormented, where I was in control, where I invited others into my space and provided for them. I needed to jumpstart the process that my brother was starting for himself.

It took me a long time to work up the nerve to bid. The stallholder claimed to have a half dozen of the sets to sell at this never-to-be-repeated price, but I waited until the conclusion of his diatribe, after he'd mentioned it was his absolute lowest offer at least ten times, before raising my hand. A box was almost thrown at me. People looked at me strangely, wondering why an alone child was bidding for crockery in the rain. I strolled away from the crowds and sat on a bale of hay, peering inside the cardboard box of riches and future that I had recently received. Beige and dull, with seventies-style flowers printed on every plate, bowl, and cup, I thought they were the most sophisticated things I'd seen. They were my ticket out. I'd be eating off of them in a place where there were buses and taxis, and I'd never have to sit in a public area for hours, cold and damp, wondering if my father had finished his liaison and when he'd come for me.

He did, of course. They both did. It was dark, the field was almost empty, and they had the audacity to claim they had truly lost me. But I knew they were lying. The fact that he didn't erupt when he saw me was immediate and conclusive evidence. And, while it does not give me pleasure to say it, he was not a particularly good actor.

I had one of those dinner service saucers until recently. During my many migrations between student flats in Glasgow and marital residences in Glasgow and London, the rest of the set was gradually damaged or given away to charity stores. But I always kept that one saucer as a talisman of my escape to maturity from my awful childhood years, and it reminded me of the exact day when I had the first inkling that I might be able to leave.

Unfortunately, the saucer did not survive my move to America, but I still see it in my memory. It still shines in my heart.

Almost forty years later, Tom is sitting across the table from me on the roof deck of my flat, visibly shaken and unable to begin the speech that he knows will shatter my existence. He stammers and has a few false starts. I ask him to simply say it. To simply tell me. I'm becoming frustrated with the waiting.

At first, he apologises because he has already informed Grant. Again, I don't understand what that implies. He says he wasn't sure how to tell me, so he asked Grant for guidance. Everything was whirring—my thoughts, Tom's speech, and the Soho skyline all around us. He finally reveals that our father called him ten days ago.

"What did me say?" I whispered. I was shaking. I had started crying. I was in Hell. "Please, Tom, please." .."

Tom glanced up at me, his blue eyes full of sadness. He gulped and then said it.

"He told me to tell you that you're not his son."

That night, I discovered something about myself that I was previously unaware of. And about a month later, one sweltering afternoon on a terrace in southern Malaysia, I was reminded of it once more: when I hear truly terrible news, my entire body tries to flee as swiftly as possible.

Before I could fully understand what Tom had said, I found myself surging backwards, knocking over the bench I was sitting on and careening away from my brother. It felt as if I needed to push this great information back, allowing myself enough room to even consider contemplating it. Sue and Dom downstairs mistook the sound they heard for Tom and me fighting, and that a body had been thrown to the floor.

"What do you mean?" I kept asking.

Tom was holding me now, attempting to calm me down. This information was so out of left field that it didn't even belong there. To say it was the last thing I expected to hear would be a huge understatement.

"You're not his son," he repeated.

Tom was also crying, but he could see how overwhelmed I was and how urgently I needed more information.

"He called me a week ago, weeping." ..," he started.

"Dad called you." ..Dad called you weeping?!" I spluttered." Nothing was making sense.

"Yes. He claimed he wouldn't tell you and would instead leave you a letter in his will. But he knew you were doing the television show, so he wanted to urge you not to embarrass yourself in public by finding out this way," he said.

Tom was wiping away tears with his thumb. I suddenly felt really sad for him. He was still my big brother and guardian. And here we were again, weeping, terrified, and clutching to one another. I thought our father had lost control over us. I was mistaken.

"Tom, find out what?! Please try to get back to me promptly. I am afraid. My heart is pounding so quickly. I think I am going to have a heart attack."

My heart was pounding so fiercely that I felt compelled to hold both hands to my chest simply to keep it inside.

"You're in shock," Tom said. "Take deep breaths."

He proceeded. "He contacted me again on Thursday and apologised for being so upset over the phone the first time. He stated that he is taking a lot of pills for his disease and believes he may have overdosed. But he wanted to ensure me, or you, that it was all true, and he was going to leave you a note in his will telling you everything, but he wants you to know now, and he says if you ask Mum, she'll deny it, but he's willing to do a DNA test. .."

"Who is my father, then?" I sobbed. Who is he?!"

Tom mentioned a name. It wasn't someone I knew, but a name I recognized as a family friend from a long time ago—in fact, from when and where I was born. Just hearing that name made things seem less abstract. Its familiarity grounded me, and I started to relax. My breathing became more regular, and my pulse dropped. This was real. It wasn't a joke intended to harm or scare me, as so many of my father's previous edicts had been. It was real.

"What else has he said?"

"He stated that he and Mum were attending a dance at the Birnam Hotel in Dunkeld. Mum was gone for a while, and this guy's wife stated he was also gone, so Dad and the wife started hunting for them. They went all over the bar and the dance floor, then went into the hotel, where they saw Mum and the guy walking out of a bedroom together.

"Then what?"

"And then nine months later you were born," he said, as if he were reading me a terrible bedtime story.

I couldn't believe my father wasn't doing this solely to hurt me. One last hurrah before he died. And how timely! How could he have thought that, Who Do You Think You Are? Would you focus on something that is spectacular, terrible, and undocumented? And then I remembered my father's experience dealing with the media, which made perfect sense. Was he really attempting to protect me for once? Of course, I reasoned that he would also be protecting himself. Going public about his cuckolding would severely damage a man's ego.

I wasn't my father's son.

It was not supposed to happen this way. Tom had discussed it with Grant, and they both agreed that I should be informed when I arrived home in New York, with Grant at my side. Tom intended to travel over in a couple of weeks, when I returned from filming in South Africa, and tell me in as quiet and protected an environment as possible. Poor Grant, on the other hand, had known this secret for the last few days we were in Cannes, keeping it to himself and never anticipating that events would force Tom to tell me so soon.

The Sunday Mail reporter had discovered my father. Once again, the tabloid press had caused turmoil in our household. Earlier that day, Tom was driving home when my father called, angry and yelling about a reporter at his front door. It's impossible to put into words how angry my father was. Even if I were dying, I'm sure it would be terrifying. Tom noticed a police car stopped on the side of the road and removed the phone from his car for a moment. When he picked it up again, our father was still complaining, but Tom told him he would handle the situation and hung up. He was terrified that our father's suspicions were right and that my Who Do You Think You Are? was about to be shot. had truly forced the news of my true lineage to be leaked, and the thought of my discovering the news by having it splattered across the front page of a newspaper scared him. He decided he needed to inform me that night and called Sue to find out what time I would arrive.

After speaking with me, he returned home and called our father to inform him that he had set the wheels in motion and was on his way to inform me of everything before I learned it through the media. Of course, this is when our father informed him that the reporter had made no mention of who my real father was and had instead requested a comment on that Times article. Our father was furious with me because I indicated he had cancer, not because this huge secret had been revealed. Tom was distraught. But it was too late; he had no choice but to proceed.

"What about mum?" I asked. "Have you spoken to her about it?"

"Not yet," replied Tom. "I wanted to let her know I was going to tell you but I didn't get a chance."

"Don't!" I blurted. "Don't talk to her until this is all sorted out in my head."

Our family has always been one of secrets, silence, and keeping things inside. The fact that my mother had never told me this, even decades after she and my father had divorced, did not surprise me. I assumed she had reasons, and whatever they were, I respected them for the time being. It seemed odd to think that my mother had strayed, yet my father's adultery had hurt me as a child. Perhaps my mother's quiet was even intended to protect my father, as we all seemed to be conditioned to do. She was the most faithful person I knew, and if they had agreed to be silent all those years ago, it was no surprise that he would be the one to break it. Although I was stunned by the news, I was also relieved that my mother had someone else in her life, someone she could love and who would ideally treat her with respect and tenderness. If I was the result of that, it couldn't be so horrible, I reasoned.

Tom told me more about what our father had said on the phone, how he suspected my mother was having an affair with this man, and how when he saw them leave the hotel room that night all those years ago, he simply said, "Well, there's no point in staying here any longer," grabbed her arm, and marched her home. It was never talked about again.

CHAPTER 5
THE CALL THAT NEVER CAME

I awoke in the white attic to find Tom gone. I lay awake for a while, too weary to move.

The day was a blur. I had lunch with Elizabeth, the director of Who Do You Think You Are?, and the only time I noticed that something was amiss was when the bill arrived.

"I just wanted to say that I understand there's going to be surprises during the shoot, but can I just put it out there that . . ." I hesitated, unsure how to express what I meant. I just needed to offer myself an exit somehow.

"I am feeling a little fragile right now. I've been travelling, and I'm tired and overwhelmed. If there's something extremely large and entirely unexpected, you'll give me a hint so I can prepare, won't you?

Elizabeth looked me in the eye, a little surprised.

"Well, of course, I can't tell you anything in advance, but I will be as respectful to you and your family's feelings as I possibly can."

That struck me as very compassionate and soothing, and it was precisely what I needed to hear. Of course, the reality was somewhat less gentle and comforting.

Saturday night was spent with my London friends, who I've known and loved for a long time but see less and less often. I was in a stupor throughout dinner, but I acted the way I wanted to be in that situation: cheerful, secure, and open. I mostly succeeded. Months later, a very sensitive friend informed me she had guessed that night that I was seriously ill. I was definitely not in my right mind.

All day, my mind had been on a steady loop of memories of insignificant events that now seemed significant. I mentally reviewed all of my childhood photos of myself and Tom and remembered how I'd always joked about our various body types—Tom, the slender boy athlete with his washboard stomach, and me, the rosy-cheeked little brother with his small belly. Now it made sense.

I swam that day, the water the ideal spot to soak up my thoughts. As I walked home, I came to a halt outside Foyles bookshop, which is located just off Charing Cross Road. I was quiet for a few moments before saying aloud, "That's why I don't have a hairy chest!"

Recently, I saw an interactive theatre work at the Brooklyn Museum. Toward the conclusion of the evening, a soft-spoken Japanese lady led me into a corner. She sat me down, put my hands in hers, and asked if I knew who I would save if the world came to an end and I could only choose one. I told her that I did. Then she asked if I believed that in similar circumstances, the person I had chosen would choose to save me. I stated that I knew they would. She looked up at me, tears in her eyes.

"You are so lucky," she said. "Some people don't even know who they would save."

One of the benefits of having been in multiple relationships before meeting Grant was that I understood a lot about myself when we met. So did he. We should have done, I think; we were both 39 at the time. So, with the euphoria and intensity of our reunion, we had a mature, honest, and forthright discourse. We're all so used to entering partnerships while concealing our baggage. Now he and I were proudly laying ours out and enjoying it. It felt great. It still does.

Grant is the nicest, funniest person I've ever met, and I've known a few nice, hilarious individuals. I feel extremely fortunate to have met him since I believe we should be together. We just work. And our eyes are the same colour. When I stare into his eyes, I feel as if I am staring at myself.

Grant woke me up on Sunday morning. He had returned home to New York, listened to the messages I had left for him, and then boarded a plane. I suddenly felt lifted. I had so many things to accomplish. With Grant arriving, I felt like I could finally take a step.

I was becoming increasingly concerned about my father's potential interview with the Sunday Mail. I had no idea how many reporters had visited his home over the years, but I had read the few printed articles for which he had provided quotes, and no one could interpret those as happy experiences, so why was he threatening to do so now? Now, at all times, when he had just declared, or rather renounced, his connection with me. Then terror began to set in. Was that what he was going to discuss? Was he going to tell the press before he even spoke to me, or before I could talk to my mother? I would not put anything past him.

But that didn't make sense. My father would never let the world know that he had been duped before he died. He! But he was terribly ill, and Tom had reported he was crying on the phone. It was all quite out of character.

Tom had spoken to our father several times in the last few days, informing him that I intended to proceed with the DNA test. He informed me that our father had begun to prevaricate and wanted to wait a few days before proceeding with any tests. Why, I thought. What was that about?

I awoke on Sunday and determined I needed to speak with the man personally. I knew I was going to have to make this decision at some point. Tom was compelled to act as a go-between for my father and myself, which was insane. This was about me and not Tom. And I could see the toll it was taking on my brother, with each upsetting interaction heightened by the need to communicate it back to me. Tom did not deserve the agony.

I asked Tom for my father's phone number and then called him. It went directly to voicemail. Understandable, I thought. He does not know my phone number. I would not answer a call from a number I did not recognize. I cleared my throat, wondering if I'd be able to say what I needed to.

The machine beeped.

"Hello, this is Alan... Cumming. I'm phoning to speak with my... to Alex Cumming. I really need to talk to him about some things that I believe he is aware of, and I would be grateful if he could call me back as soon as possible.

I thought I was going to hang up, but I ended up talking more.

"It is urgent. It is quite urgent, so please call me as soon as possible. "Thank you."

I gave my number and hung up. And the wait began.

Tom informed me that my father was recovering from a surgery. He was plainly at home. In reality, Tom had spoken with him that morning, telling him to expect my call. As the minutes became hours, the fact that he was purposefully not calling me back irritated me more and more. He once again wielded absolute power. He couldn't help himself, I thought. He was used to keeping me weak, vulnerable, and frightened. Though I suspected that some of his reluctance to engage with me stemmed from his own trepidation. I wasn't afraid of him anymore, and I believe it scared him.

I called again at 7 p.m. No response.

My father's silence was preventing me from exiting the hole he had just dug for me. I felt as if I was back on the estate, waiting for him to check me, but this time I was angry and frustrated rather than anxious. I wanted it to be over.

I began to think about how I would handle this scenario if he never spoke to me. Grant had told me I didn't need him to perform a DNA test because men pass along identical Y chromosomes to all of their male progeny. Tom and I could do a test, and if the Y chromosomes did not match, it would be conclusive evidence that my father's story was real.

So we discovered the kits on the Internet and scheduled their delivery for a night when I would be back in England. Tom would come to my house and we would take the test. I felt compelled to wait until my father called, but exhaustion eventually won out. I was incredibly exhausted, but I was also a little concerned that I would appear on camera the next morning looking so raddled. There was no makeup or hair stylist available for this shoot, and no one could hide the impact of anything I'd learnt. This was normal, baby, and I despised myself for not being more demanding.

As we climbed the stairs into the sleeping loft, I informed Grant that whatever occurred, I needed to know the truth for myself. If my father only gave me the information he had passed on through Tom, I was going to make it my duty to get to the bottom of the matter, even if it meant going to see my true father. I went to sleep again, like I had so many times as a child, knowing full well that I could never rely on my father.

I was forty-five years old. I'd been waiting for a phone call from my father since I was twenty-nine, my age when we last spoke.

I suppose I should have known what to expect.

CHAPTER 6
CONVERSATIONS IN THE SNOW

It was between Christmas and New Year, and everything was quiet and white. We had received an unusually huge snowfall, which made me thrilled. The snow signalled that everything had settled down. My father's attention was drawn away from the usual, from me, to the effects of the snow and the state of the local roads. The estate workers were granted days off until the snow cleared, and my typical schedule of tasks, aside from shovelling and bringing in logs, was postponed. It was actually acceptable to do some lolling.

I adored the sound of the snow. It was both peaceful and echoey, and its presence made the world feel safer.

My mother and I were watching television. Suddenly, the front door was pushed open, and my father's voice rang out for my mother. Mum and I jumped up, horrified. It sounded like he was hurt or being hunted. She arrived at the living room door before me, but I caught a glimpse of my father, who was swaying slightly as he made his way to the front room, which we rarely used except for visitors or on Christmas. Behind him, I noticed Mr. Shaw, the head gamekeeper, with whom my father had clearly been drinking.

My father was not a drinker by any means. Like most Scotsmen, he enjoyed a drink, but I rarely saw him in anything more than "a bit merry," so seeing him like this suddenly was rather shocking. I blamed both Mr. Shaw and the snow. The former was known to enjoy a drink a bit too much, while the latter created an environment in which boredom and access to a beverages cabinet may lead to the current predicament.

We want whisky, woman!"My father yelled as he sped past.

My mother slammed the door, leaving me in the living room to worry what would come of their muffled, yet intense tones. A few minutes later, my mother dashed back into the room and headed for the kitchen.

"The cheek of the man," she murmured over her shoulder, before reappearing with a jug of water, probably to be combined with whisky in the front room.

"Coming in here and shouting at me like that."

Just then, Tom arrived home. He asked what had happened, and I told him.

"Dad's drunk."

"Drunk?", said Tom. "In the afternoon?"

"He's been at Mr. Shaw's house and now they've come here because they ran out of whisky."

Suddenly, the sounds at the other end of the house became louder, and the front door opened and closed. I waited for the customary cold airflow to pass through to us under the living room door. Mr. Shaw must have returned home. My parents' screams escalated to a crescendo, and they both entered the living room, my mother angry by her husband's actions, and my father weary, foggy, and bemused.

"Get upstairs, boys," he mumbled.

"What makes you think you can come in here and shout at me like that, asking for whisky like I'm your servant?" I heard my mother say, firm and outraged, as the kitchen door closed behind us.

"I'll come in here any way I want," said my father. "This is my house."

Tom raced me up the stairs and won, as usual. The "Big Room" where we went to complete our studies and play games was quite cold. We attempted to pass the time by reading and joking around, but we were both privately concerned about what was going on downstairs.

Mum was unusually feisty. It indicated a shift in her attitude toward our father, and while it made me nervous, I enjoyed it. She had just started working in the office of a grain mill in the nearby village. She was discovering herself again.

Initially, my father was highly opposed to her taking the position. For several years, she had been taking night classes at Tom's high school to earn certifications that would allow her to return to work. This did not sit well with my father, who was continually trying to sabotage or impede her progress.

The most blatant and cruel illustration of this occurred one spring evening when my father ordered Tom and me to follow him to the field below our house and assist him in catching one of our sheep that was about to lamb. As was customary on such occasions, our father would instruct us to stand behind a hedgerow and then chase the agitated ewe towards us, yelling obscenities if we failed to seize its horns and drag it to the ground as it rushed past us in terror for its life. He basically treated us like sheepdogs, frequently whistling commands and expecting us to comprehend what he meant. That night, we had finally caught the unfortunate sheep and were about to seal the pen to give it some rest when our mother came at the top of the field, dressed for her night lesson.

"That puts me away!" she said, then quickly turned on her heels to return through the garden gates and into her car. I could tell my father's attitude was changing seeing her like this, so it came as no surprise when I heard him cry out to my mother's back, "Get down here! We need help!"

"I have my classes, Ali," she said, half assertively, half pleading.

"The animal is in anguish. Get down here!"

It occurred to me that any tension was most likely caused by the fact that the sheep was heavily pregnant and we had just been making it gallop around the field for the past half hour. I could tell it only needed to relax, lie down, and continue its work.

Our mother arrived in the pen through the mud and mounds of sheep dung.

"I'll be late, Ali," she said.

My father ignored her and focused on us and the sad sheep.

"Get in here and help us hold down this beast," he commanded calmly and threateningly. Tom and I stared at Mum, wondering what she would do. What could she do? She set down her folders and notebooks and clambered over the gate to join us.

Our father made us hold down the sheep and instructed my mother to assist it in giving birth. This means she had to insert her arm into its uterus and extract the young lamb. This is not an unusual practice throughout the country. Because I had the smallest hands, I frequently found myself doing this. But this time, we were all aware that it was completely unnecessary.

"You'd better get going, then," my father mocked her when she finally rose up, her face speckled and her good blouse soaked in blood.

But Mum persisted, and when the job came up in the granary's office, she managed to persuade my father that it would not interfere with his household "requirements." In fact, I offered to help even more with getting the tea ready each night, ensuring that my father's regulated existence would not be disturbed. This employment felt like the beginning of something good.

"Boys! Tea is ready."

Tom and I stared at each other. We both wondered what awaited us downstairs. Mum sounded wonderful, even confident. But where was our dad? We hadn't heard a door slam to indicate that he had left, so he must still be in the kitchen, and given the yelling match we'd witnessed before, what foul mood would emanate from him now?

We both came to a halt as we stepped into the kitchen. My father was sitting at the kitchen table next to me, as usual, but he was leaning forward, his head and arms stretched across the top. He was out cold. And my mother had arranged the table for our evening meal around him.

"Come on, it's all right, he won't wake up," Mum murmured, knowing my fear. It seemed like I was entering the sleeping ogre's den. Tom laughed.

"Are we going to enjoy our tea while he just lies there?He asked.

"Yes," Mum replied calmly. "Your father doesn't seem to be hungry, but we all need to eat."

So we sat down and uncomfortably passed the butter and condiments over my father while eating our meals. I looked up and noticed that his eyes had opened and were staring directly at me. Panic overcame me, but he simply swallowed, smacked his lips, and closed his eyes again.

After a while, I started to love the Alice-in-Wonderland-like sensation. We all did. In his drunken state, our father posed no threat to us, nor did he impede the continuation of our daily routine. Sitting at that table night after night seemed terrible. It would happen again tomorrow, no one knew, but today, with my father snoring and us passing the biscuit plate over his head, we could rest peacefully.

Later, when we'd washed the dishes and cleared the table, my mother suggested we travel to Dundee to see Jaws, the new picture that everyone was raving about. I could not believe my ears. I could count on one hand how many times we had gone to the movies as a family, or part of a family. In a frenzy of excitement, I hurried upstairs to change. Everything was shifting that night. The prospect of driving all the way to Dundee in the snow to attend a movie was thrilling enough, but doing it while our father lay asleep in the darkness of the kitchen was absolutely breathtaking. And the fact that my mother acted calmly and confidently added to the sweetness.

Tom asked if he might cycle to Monikie to see his girlfriend instead of joining us. Mum agreed. It seemed like anything was possible tonight!

We took off in the car, and after a few minutes of driving over the crisp moonlit country roads, Mum spoke up.

"What do you think, Alan, about you, me, and Tommy living on our own?"

I felt as if the skies had opened, bringing light, warmth, and goodness into the car. I felt God. It was almost too much. This afternoon, everything was usual. The snow had provided a temporary respite, but suddenly it seemed as if the entire world had altered. I wanted to cry, laugh, run across the bench, and kiss my mother. But I was paralyzed. My mouth felt dry, and I could barely hear myself speak. .."Away from Dad, you mean?"

I just wanted to make sure.

"Yes, away from dad. Just you, me, and Tommy live together. Would you like that?"

"Yes," I replied, a tear falling down my cheek. "I would like that."

Suddenly, the car hit a piece of ice, and we spun out of control for what seemed like an eternity. I believed we would both perish. The God I had glimpsed minutes previously turned out to be less kind. He was the same old God, the one who crushed your hopes and held you in check. He was the angry, vengeful man of God, and my mother had dared to cross him.

By the time the automobile had stopped, we were facing back the direction we had come, and my side of the car was leaning into a ditch. The engine was turned off, and all I could hear was our terrified breathing and my pulse pounding madly in my small bony chest. After a few moments, Mum inquired as to my well-being, to which I replied quietly. She restarted the engine, and we continued on our journey, but this time quietly and meekly, with neither triumph or elation.

The subject was never discussed again.

I looked down at my notes. I had created a list with designated spots for me to scribble down his responses. I needed to recall every detail of this talk.

"Are you sure?" Are you completely sure?"I attempted to seem bland and scientific.

"I'd never have brought it up if I wasn't certain, Alan," my father added. "I wrote you a letter about it some years ago. It is in my will. But when I heard you were performing this TV show, I didn't want you to find out in that way, so I phoned Tom."

The following question proved tough to ask. I was born on January 27, 1965, and I needed mathematics to make sense. I needed everything to make sense, so I said it.

"Are you confident you didn't have sex with Mum in April or May 1964?"

"No, Alan. No." Sex had been intermittent with your mother for some time prior to then." Okay, that was way more than I wanted to hear. A simple "no" might have sufficed, but his openness inspired me instead.

"That is why we had to move away from Dunkeld, Alan," my father explained.

"Why?"

"The shame," he remarked. There it was. I knew it would rear its ugly head soon.

"Is it a pity that Mum had sex with someone else?" I inquired, wondering if he, like me, had anticipated how this conversation would unfold and if he thought we'd go this deep so quickly.

"The shame of people knowing," he stepped back slightly.

"I was compromised in my work because I had dealings with him."

It made sense. We relocated from Dunkeld to the west coast of Scotland, near Fort William, when I was just under a year old, and stayed there until I was four, when we moved to Panmure Estate. And I remembered enough from my childhood to understand how a small rural village like Dunkeld could be miserable when everyone knew you had dirty laundry.

This also helped to explain why my father was so open about his mistresses as we grew up. Did he want my mother to feel the same agony, shame, and slight on his masculinity that he'd carried throughout the first year of my existence, pain that hurt so much that he relocated his young family across the nation to start a new life away from it?

"Does my real father know?" I moved on.

"Oh, he knows. He must know. You know, he and his wife had a child, I believe a son, immediately after your birth—"

"Wait, what?"I hadn't really considered the new siblings issue. I mean, I assumed my true father had other children, but having a half brother my age was something else.

"Was his wife pregnant at the same time as Mum?"I asked.

"They had a few further children, but she divorced him. Then, well. .His words faded off to silence.

"What?"I wish he would simply tell me. Each silence felt like a booby trap. I couldn't trust him.

"So, he tried to shoot himself," my father remarked.

So yet another man had found the maze of my family and decided that the only way out was to put a pistol to his head. This did not bode well. This was an episode from Dallas.

But he lived?"I finally got out.

"Oh, absolutely. He missed. His relatives had taken him away. "He is fine now."

"Has he remarried?"I pondered. The cast of my life's new characters was expanding.

"He has a partner. I'm not sure if they ever married," he said.

I looked down at my list of questions. We were moving through them quickly. Perhaps they moved too quickly. For a little moment, emotion rose to the surface, and I had to swallow it down. I paused. "Sorry, it's just a lot to take in," I responded, recovering.

And, in that short second of thought, my father pounced.

"I can imagine," he responded calmly. "I've had those reporter fellows at my door a few times saying things that were a shock to me."

Oh, I'm sorry; I thought we were talking about how I've thought you were my father for forty-five years when you aren't. I had no idea we were back to talking about you and how the press had abused you. Sorry.

His narcissism had no boundaries.

I responded, "You know, I'm very sorry you've had to deal with anything like that, but I believe that if you knew me better, or even if you knew how to contact me, you could have contacted me and I'd have told you how to deal with them. And I could have told you that what they were saying was incorrect."

I didn't want to be diverted. I still had a lot more to ask. But it was as if my father did not hear me.

"I've had them outside my door several times over the years, always asking for my response to something you've said." .."he continued.

"Do you know what, Dad?"

I addressed him as "Dad" for the first time. This was a mistake. I had purposely restrained myself till now, but it simply came out. It made me feel weak and like a little child again. "I understand. I really do. I deal with the media every day of my life. All I'm saying is that the fact that I'm not in your life is not just why they're there in the first place, but also why you're unsure how to deal with them.

"They ring my doorbell and ask for a comment." ."He was not listening. I had to turn it up a notch.

Listen to me! This is not what we are discussing today! But I want you to know that I have always been truthful to the press. Sometimes the truth hurts, and sometimes they manipulate and distort it, but I've never said anything to them with the aim of harming you."

I halted. There was silence on the line. I took the initiative. I realised I had a limited period of time before my father would be of no assistance to me. I was that small child back on the estate, trying to decide whether I could calm him down or if it was only a matter of time until I was hit. Only tonight he wouldn't hit me; instead, he withheld what he knew I needed more than anything else: the truth. He had complete control over everything, which he enjoyed.

I looked down at the next item on my list and asked, "Who else knows?"

He listed an old acquaintance of my mother's who he believed had been informed, but he couldn't be certain. His sister had brought up the matter before her death. Of course, there was the woman he was now living with, the wife of the suicide and the grandchild who was looking for autographs. My real father's wife, of course. He stated he had run across her from time to time over the years, and while he could tell she was aware, they had never discussed it.

"Had Mum been having an affair with him for a while?" I hoped she had been—she needed loving attention, and I prayed she had received it. But if my existence was only due to a brief moment of affection, that was OK too.

"Well, I do remember not long before all of this, I was asked to start taking Tommy to football practice on Saturday afternoons." For the first time, his tone was angry.

"And do you think she saw him on those afternoons?" I prodded.

"I couldn't say for sure."

"But do you think so?"

"Yes, I've got a pretty good idea."

We talked about what happened that night again. The dance took place at the Birnam Hotel in Dunkeld. Mum had been gone for a bit when the man's wife arrived and reported that her husband was also missing. They headed off together through the busy dance floor, back through the bar, and into the hotel. As they climbed the stairs, a door opened, and my mother came, with the man behind her. They exchanged glances for a time before he grabbed my mother's wrist, muttered, "There's no point in staying here any longer," and yanked her away.

"And you never spoke about it again. Ever?" I asked.

"Well, once, years later at Panmure, it nearly came up."

My father paused, recalling the scene, and then, as if he hadn't thought about it in decades, remarked, "It was on your birthday, funnily enough."

I sat astonished in silence.

I gazed outside the window. We were approaching one of those northern towns. Lancaster, was it? Or York. York is most likely the answer.

"You must have known, Alan."

"What?" For a brief period, the train and everything came to a halt.

"Come on!" You must've known!" He seemed almost joyful, as if we had advanced to the "We can laugh about it now" stage of the story. We hadn't.

I was dumbfounded.

"How could I have known?"

My father cleared his throat before pausing for effect.

"Didn't you realise that we never bonded?" he stated. It felt as if he were explaining the solution to a riddle to me.

I sputtered.

Again, he spoke. "Have you ever wondered why we didn't bond?"

Everything sped up. My vision was filled with millisecond memories from years ago: my father's furious and crazy face, the stinging his hands left on me, the humiliation, and the misery.

I wanted to shout that, sure, I had pondered why we hadn't bonded, but it wasn't because he wasn't my real father. But I could not. I was literally startled.

The train was going, my heart was racing, and my father was waiting for an answer at the end of the line.

I felt out of my depth when interacting with this man.

And suddenly I got it.

He was telling me to accept that his actions against me were justifiable because I was not of his blood. He urged me to accept my own physical and psychological torment.

"Of course, I've noticed we never bonded," I said. "But I wasn't sure why. "I assumed you were just an angry, unhappy man," I said softly.

"Why haven't you divorced Mum?" I asked immediately. I felt like the elevator doors were about to close, and I was seizing my final chance before this conversation ended.

"I couldn't do that," he replied impatiently. "I had kids to bring up."

Yes, I understand. I was one of them.

We'd been conversing for a while, and I'd asked all of my questions.

I wasn't sure how you ended up having this conversation, but I knew my father wasn't going to be the one to do it. And I was finished.

"You know," I continued, "when I think about your relationship, you were always the one who had open affairs, and I always puzzled why Mum didn't protest more about it. Is it because she thought she couldn't complain because she had the first affair that wrecked your marriage?"

There was a significant halt. I felt I had gone too far.

"Well, I can't speak for your mother," he added finally, "but sometimes people stay together for their children. They make sacrifices for others. And your mother and I waited until you were both out of the home to separate."

Oh my, here we go with the usual "We stayed together for you kids" routine. So, not only was I accountable for my own maltreatment because of my newfound half-breed status, but the fact that it lasted for so long was owing to my abuser's goodwill and self-sacrifice? Great.

My entire body felt on the verge of explosion, collapse, or conflagration. I had one final inquiry.

"So, where does my true father live now?" I asked.

It was as if I had pressed the ignition button. My father was suddenly years younger, and snarled with the force and rage of the man that plagued me:

"Don't you go bothering him!"

I was shocked back into my seat. I knew I needed to remain cool since the man shouting at me was not rational and his default mode of communication was shouting. I must not give him any reason to believe I attacked him.

"I won't bother him. But I only found out three days ago that he is my father, so I believe I have the right to ask a few questions about him."

Silence.

"Don't you, dad?"

He ignored my question but did provide me some information about where this individual now lived. My father believed he ran a pub or a garage. I pondered if I'd ever meet him or my half-siblings. I wondered what they would be like.

I informed my father that I was going forward with the DNA test.

"I'm not sending a swab to America!" was the response. He was enraged now.

"Well, you don't need to." I described how Tom and I would conduct the test ourselves. I'd get in touch once I had the results. I could tell that the wind had blown out of his sails. Withholding his DNA was his final trump card. Now he had to wait.

I set the phone down next to my paper and pen, clenched my hands together, and let my body shake. My teeth began to rattle, my watch slammed on the table's surface, and my knees moved reflexively. Sunny England rushed past. I gathered myself together and walked back a few carriages to meet the BBC crew.

CHAPTER 7
SILENT ECHOES

I'm at peace. I'm twelve years old, my jeans are around my ankles, and I've just made a major discovery.

I'm resting on my back on a grassy clearing that protrudes over a gully in the woodland, with the burn below tinkling its way to the North Sea. I come here every night after we finish our tea. This is partly to escape the solitude of my parents' house, but largely to avoid my father and, more recently, to appreciate what I've discovered my penis is capable of. It appears to serve some purpose.

If I bend my head towards the burn and press one ear into the grass, I may hear birds tweeting and possibly a faraway cow or sheep in the other. It's a quiet spring night, brisk and hopeful. I know if I lie here for too long, I'll fall asleep and wake up chilly, with flakes on my abdomen where I now feel wet and warm. I open my eyes.

There is a man standing there, looking at me. He is on the route at the top of the hill, which travels along the edge of the forest before dropping down to the gully level. He isn't close enough to be physically dangerous, but he's clearly just witnessed me ejaculate, and I recognize this man. He's one of the estate's forestry workers and works for my father. Every day, I see him as I walk through the sawmill yard to catch the school bus. When he realises I'm looking at him, he pulls back onto the path and disappears. My heart is beating, and my cheeks are red again. I can sense something stirring within me. I'm automatically resisting, but it's battling hard for control of me. It's a shame.

What did I do wrong? I ask myself. I understand that boys do this. I understand that it is both inevitable and normal. I didn't know how nice it would feel. So, why do I feel apprehensive about doing what is right? Why should I feel horrible only because this man saw me? Why? Because he might tell my father, and like so many others before him, this newfound bliss will be imprinted on.

I lie there in the dusk for a while before making a decision, little understanding how it will affect every aspect of my life and every fibre of my being for the rest of my life: I refuse to be ashamed. This man was in the wrong. He was the voyeur, although accidentally.

But I did not wish him ill. I'd have done the same. I even imagined my father would be relieved to learn that some progress was being made in my stumbling road to manhood. So I rejected shame.

I went to pull up my jeans but decided against it and lay back down, staring up at the darker sky. I closed my eyes.

By 6 A.M. I was looking out of my hotel room window onto the ancient Dundee docks. I was very sleepy, yet my thoughts refused to let me sleep. In just a few hours, I would see my mother.

I was concerned that she would know something was amiss. I felt like there was a sign above my head that said "MAN IN TROUBLE." I wanted to ask so many questions but couldn't, especially in front of a TV crew. After all, today's discoveries and disclosures weren't going to be about me or my biological father. I had to try to put all of it aside and act normal. I needed to act.

No matter what is going on in my personal life, I know how to block it out when working. Whether I have good news, bad news, am hungover, joyful, or sick, it is part of an actor's duty to be able to neutralise it all and become whatever the character needs to feel. Today was no exception: I'd play the part of Alan Cumming, a cheeky chappie sipping tea with his mother and going through old family photos and mementos, as the audience expected. It shouldn't need much of me. However, when the light began to slowly slip across the water's surface, I wondered if I was up to it.

I went to the gym, hoping that the endorphins might temporarily relieve the buzzing in my head. I met the team for breakfast and soon we were off, recording in the car as I drove along the coast road to my mother's house.

I talked about my mother while driving, which was filmed by the camera directed at me from the passenger seat. I mentioned how much I admire her, how she has dealt with the changes in my life, and how much she has matured as a person over the years. I also mentioned that she still has the power to surprise me. That was an understatement given what had happened over the last few days.

When we arrived at Mary Darling's house, Elizabeth, the director, and the soundman rushed over to put a microphone on her and block her from seeing me, ensuring that our reunion on camera was completely unplanned.

I could see my mother straining to peer over their shoulders to see me. I could tell she was quite excited. I imagine she hadn't slept well the night before, but for different reasons.

Soon after hugging on her porch, we entered her living room and proceeded to set up what would be the main topic of the conversation: what my mother knew about her father.

As the team set up some lighting and Mum and Elizabeth discussed what she was going to say and show me, I began scouring the walls and shelves of her lounge for photos of my family. Tom and I were kids, dressed in swimming trunks, on a jetty in Panmure's garden after a boat trip. Then came college, weddings, and holidays. Naturally, my father was not present. My mother abandoned him when I was twenty and away at theatre school in Glasgow. She had worked hard to become financially independent of him, and just when I believed they had reached an amicable condition of living completely separate lives under the same roof, she called and stated she would be moving to a different address from now on. For many years, I had wished for my parents to divorce, but when I learned the news, I was taken aback, surprised, and strangely upset. It was as if all of my pent-up anguish from observing two individuals in such a miserable partnership poured out of me. I suppose I didn't understand how much I wanted their relationship to work. I wished for a proper mother and father with a normal connection. And it became evident that this would never happen.

Looking at these photographs from my entire life, it wasn't hard to imagine I had a different father. A strange peace settled on me, and I just knew.

"So, Mum, what do you remember about your father?" I asked her.

She was nervous and careful as she spoke. It only made me love her more. She mentioned how little she knew about the man, other than that he had served in the military as a Cameron Highlander. He was stationed in Inverness, where he met my grandmother.

Tommy Darling married in 1937, at the age of twenty. Mary Darling was born a year later, and her three brothers arrived in fast succession. Despite having a growing family, Tommy Darling's visits home were increasingly infrequent. In previous conversations about him, I had questioned my mother why she believed he had returned home so little, and she explained that it was typical during the war for a soldier's leave to be cancelled or postponed. That made sense, I think, but surely a five-year delay was a bit excessive?

I asked Mum where her father had gone after the war. "Well, he visited numerous places. "He was in France and Burma," she explained.

"What did he do?" I asked. I didn't even know this basic fact about him.

He was a motorcyclist, a courier who relayed information between battalions on the battlefield. Mum then showed me a pewter mug that he owned. It was one of the few items she owned that had once belonged to Tommy Darling. According to the inscription, he won the cup in a service motorcycling test in 1939.

"So he is a biker?" I joked. Tommy Darling's image was forming in my head, and he was certainly pushing my notions.

She also had his Certificate of Service, which I read aloud.

"Excellent type. Honest and sober. ." I looked up to Mum. "This is rare for our family!"

I beg your pardon!" she joked back.

Mum then proudly showed me the medal he had gotten for bravery in the field. I had seen it as a child, but I had no idea when or why Tommy Darling was known in this way.

We discussed the circumstances of his death. He joined the Malayan police force in 1950, and died less than a year later. Mary Darling was thirteen and hadn't seen her father since she was eight. When I gently inquired about the circumstances surrounding his death, my mother calmly recounted the narrative as it had been shared with her. He'd been cleaning a gun. There was still one round in the chamber. He had accidently shot himself.

This was new to me. I'd always assumed he'd been shot inadvertently on a shooting range by a stray bullet, becoming a victim of that wonderfully oxymoronic phrase "friendly fire." I suppose my boyish imagination must have dreamed it up.

The storyline was clearly thickening.

As the interview concluded, I smiled at her and kissed her. I know Mum had been nervous, but she did an excellent job. As she scampered through to the kitchen to begin serving the lunch she'd cooked for me and the crew, I took a moment to reflect on how similar our current situations were—both of us on the verge of discovering the truth about our fathers. I got a flash of having to tell her what my father had disclosed, and how her face would crumple if I did, but I put that notion aside for the time being.

"Alan! Will you pour these people a glass of wine instead of just sitting there?" My mother cautioned me. My reverie was disturbed, and I returned to my role as obedient son.

The next stage in my investigation was to dive deeper into Tommy Darling's military career, so I arrived at the National Library of Scotland, a stunning edifice situated off Edinburgh's Royal Mile, a few hours later. I had actually filmed there the year before for a documentary about the Scottish sense of humor, and I was delighted to learn from one of its ancient tomes that we Scots were the first to catalog the term fuck! Now here I was again, going over Tommy Darling's military records and documentation with a military historian by my side.

The first thing that struck me was why my grandfather chose to join the Cameron Highlanders over a battalion closer to his home. I discovered that the Highlanders had a strong reputation for being a loyal, close-knit bunch of soldiers. Thinking back on my grandfather's orphanhood, I wondered whether he was looking for a family in the military. A lump grew in the back of my throat.

Wow. This was going to be harder than I expected. Pouring my attention on learning about my grandfather's life as a means of momentarily escaping my own past was not going to work, especially since everything I learned was relevant to how I was feeling and my experiences. I began to see why my grandfather was such an absent father. His family experience was so limited that he may never fully understand it.

Tommy Darling was stationed in Inverness and served as a cook in the barracks. His military records created a picture of an ideal soldier.

Indeed, the only negative in any of his documents during this period was that one night he was stopped by a military police officer and fined for riding his motorcycle with insufficient light on his licence plate.

I looked at Tommy Darling and my grandmother's wedding photos, recognized my great-auntie Ina as a bridesmaid, and began to form an image of the young, newly married cook, soon to be a father for the first time, full of optimism for the future, and forming the family he never had.

Then everything changed.

When war broke out in 1939, Tommy Darling extended his military service by volunteering as a dispatch rider for the Royal Army Ordnance Corps. Suddenly, I remembered the initials RAOC on the pewter mug. I handed it to the historian, who inspected it and informed me that Tommy Darling received the mug for winning a trial, which is a test of a motorcyclist's ability to go cross-country under conditions similar to those found in battle. And he would soon be experiencing actual battle, as the Cameron Highlanders were transferred to France and sent to the front lines of World battle II in 1940.

As I looked through images and descriptions of the Allied efforts, I realised exactly what a dispatch rider would have done in battle. I also realised Tommy Darling was a bit of a daredevil. In the space of a few hours, I learned that he had left the comfort of the battalion depot kitchens (and his family) to serve his country in the most perilous conditions imaginable—tearing through the mud of the French countryside delivering critical messages from military headquarters to the troops on the front lines. He had suddenly transformed from a man in a uniform on my New York wall to a swashbuckling adventurer.

In 1940, the Germans had completely defeated the Allied forces and forced them to retreat, and the huge evacuation from Dunkirk in Normandy was being prepared rapidly. I discovered that the Cameron Highlanders were stationed forty miles south of Dunkirk in a last-ditch effort to block the German advance and allow the evacuation to proceed. Tommy Darling was riding his dispatch bike between battalion headquarters in Violaine and La Bassée, where the Camerons were attempting to prevent a 300-strong tank division from crossing the canal and approaching Dunkirk. It was at this period that he received the Military Medal that my mother had shown me. The historian presented me the citation from Tommy's regimental records:

Lance Corporal Darling showed extraordinary daring and disregard for his own safety in getting communications to the advanced Companies.

I wanted to learn more. Tommy Darling was becoming more real to me, and I sensed an unspoken bond developing. It was a concern for a man I'd never met. But that's all there was.

Sensing my yearning for more, the historian added, "This is a gallantry award for which you should be very proud."

However, something else was disclosed that struck a deeper chord with me. Tommy Darling's Military Medal was such a prestigious prize that he was invited to Buckingham Palace in 1941 to receive it. Sixty-eight years later, I, his grandson, had also visited Buckingham Place to collect a medal. In the 2009 Queen's Honors List, I received the OBE (Officer of the British Empire) for "services to film, theatre, and the arts, as well as activism for equal rights for the gay and lesbian community," which was a little less brave and valiant than my grandfather's, but still an honour.

My mother, brother, and spouse all came to the palace with me that day. Mary Darling was brimming with joy and pride like a little girl in a fairy tale, a feathered fascinator perched on her head as she sat between Tom and Grant in the first row waiting for me to emerge to get my award. It's astonishing that none of us realised Tommy Darling had been there nearly seven decades before us.

The group left to photograph the Edinburgh scenery, and I returned to my accommodation in Edinburgh's New Town alone. It was one of those boutique hotels made up of multiple buildings, and I stayed in the attic suite. As I started my bath, I opened the windows and enjoyed the vista that stretched all the way to the Firth of Forth, as well as the breeze that came up from the coast. I appeared fatigued. When I had moments alone, I worried that the toll of everything was too great to endure.

I closed my eyes and focused on the hum of traffic coming up to Haymarket Station or down to Stockbridge. I could not get the sight of a photograph on my mother's wall out of my mind. It dates back to when we lived in Dunkeld. The image was of myself, my mother, and Tom. I'm just a baby; I'm standing, but only as a baby. Tom and I appear to be friendly. Not siblings.

CHAPTER 8
THE PAST IN PIECES

When I was nineteen, my mother eventually abandoned my father.

I was in my final year of drama school in Glasgow, but I was granted permission to leave for a term to make my professional theatre debut as Malcolm in the Tron Theatre's production of Macbeth. On my twentieth birthday, my mother travelled down to Glasgow to see me, and we had lunch and spent the afternoon together. Two days later, I was astonished to hear her voice when I answered the phone at my flat.

"Is everything alright, Mum?" I asked.

"Oh yeah, pet. I'm just phoning to let you know that starting April 21st, I'll be living at 16 Brook Street in Monifieth."

There was silence on the line. I couldn't fully grasp what I had heard.

"Um, what?" I finally succeeded.

"As of the twenty-first of April I will be residing at sixteen Brook Street, Monifieth," she stated. "I've bought a wee flat and I will get the keys in six weeks."

"How about Dad?" I inquired, still puzzled.

"Oh, he'll be staying at Panmure."

"Are you abandoning him?"

"Well, Alan, you know your father and I have been living separate lives for quite some time," I heard my little mother explain.

My legs suddenly gave way under me, and I was sitting on the floor, screaming like a baby. Of course, I knew it would be good for everyone involved, especially my mother, but it still surprised me. I was quite upset. Not so much about the breakup itself, but more the realisation of how much of my youth had been spent longing for it to happen. The eventual pronouncement rang more like a bell of pain from my past than a clanging of change in my present.

At this moment, relations in the Cumming household were nearly friendly. My parents appeared to be satisfied in their separate lives, with no resentment, and I imagined that my father's wrath and lack of regard for his wife and family had been tempered, if not shrivelled, by age. Of course, I later discovered that this détente was the result of a mutual agreement to separate signed a few years earlier. At twenty, I was thought capable of dealing with the shock of having divorced parents.

A few weeks after my mother informed me of the news, I travelled to Panmure for the weekend. I understood that was the final time I'd ever sleep in my childhood home. From that point forward, I had no intention of returning back save for a brief visit to see my father. I would never stay the night again. Knowing this, I moved through the rooms, seeing them in a different light. I was melancholy for something that had just ended, possibly because I had wished it would end for so long.

I had already taken most of the items I intended to keep when I first came to Glasgow a few years ago. For me, that shift was more than just a college semester; it was permanent. I might return for visits at Christmas and the occasional weekend, but I would never return permanently. My mother, unbeknownst to me, was plotting the same escape.

My mother invited me to visit her new flat and informed me of the purchases she was making. I could tell she was excited for this new chapter in her life. I understood.

My father was present during meals. He went out as usual for the evening, but he was not missed, and there was no hatred or offence taken from his absence, nor was his demeanour confrontational or threatening, as it had been for so many years. I saw this tranquillity as a positive thing. My father had stopped being a physical menace to me when I left and started living my own life; he had even become very courteous. This transformation in him enabled me to store much of my past in a box that I never wanted to uncover. For ten years, I kept it hidden, believing that my family was no more difficult or demanding than everyone else's. I didn't start to forgive my father— far from it. However, as I went about my future business, I began to forget about him. My father had grown less humorous, but during dinner at the kitchen table, I could tell him and my mother about my new, odd life at college, and he would chuckle. When he took me to the train station, he would shake my hand and pass me a ten or twenty-pound note, telling me to use it to buy a drink for myself and my friends.

That last weekend, which had been filled with my mother's excitement and hope for the future, concluded with a silent drive to the Dundee train station in my father's car. He had never mentioned or referenced the idea that Mum was departing in a week or so. He had never told me anything about how things might alter. He'd said nothing at all. My mother had spoken with him about some of the logistics of her move, but he exhibited no emotion or concern. I suppose I felt bad for him that weekend. I was truly worried about him.

In the darkness of the car that Sunday night, I finally mustered the confidence to say, "Dad, we haven't talked about Mum leaving, and I'm just a little anxious about how you're going to get along, you know, look after yourself and everything. Don't you think you might need some assistance?"

Nothing. There was nothing nasty or angry off about it.

"I mean, don't you think you should maybe get someone to come and help you a bit," I said. "To do some cooking, ironing, and stuff?"

"I don't need anyone to do my cooking and ironing," the enigmatic reply said.

Little did I know that as soon as my mother had packed her car for the final voyage to her new home and wished my father well, his lover—she of the suicide husband and the improper autograph request at my grandmother's funeral—would take her place. And thus my father was correct: he didn't need somebody to do his cooking or ironing.

I awoke in Lille after another restless night of sleep. I had eaten alone in my hotel room because the crew needed to go grab some location shots before the sun set. As much as I knew I needed alone time to process everything that was going on and give myself permission to express my emotions, I also craved company. I Skyped with Grant back in London, which provided little relief. It was wonderful to be able to see him rather than simply hear him, and for that I am grateful to contemporary technology. However, seeing the one you love but unable to touch them, when their comfort is what you desire the most, makes you feel worse and more depleted than if you had not seen them at all. As Macbeth puts it, "'Twas a rough night."

The following day, I found myself waiting. As is common in the film and television industries, one spends a significant amount of time waiting for filming to begin. My current location was a flat, open ploughed area between the villages of Violaine and La Bassée. I stood waiting for the crew to set up and plan how to film the upcoming reveal. I was asked to perform endless walking shots for prospective voiceovers. All I wanted to know was what made Tommy Darling such a hero, and I was standing next to a small historian who was dying to tell me, but nothing could be spoken until we were in the best position to hear the revelation and properly capture my reaction.

I realised I was imprisoned in a genealogical aspic, both in real life and on television. Both of us were kept waiting for the truth.

Tommy Darling's medal only read "Bravery in the Field," but the drive to Buckingham Palace and the crew's talking and preparation for the news I was about to hear made it clear that it was a far bigger thing than it sounded.

Finally, this tiny historian, David, was released from his leash. He began telling me the story of how my grandfather received his medal. The 1st Cameron Highlanders, my grandfather's battalion, were defending La Bassée from the Germans. David pointed to the right, back along the road that led us to this field.

David was clearly excited about the story, just as I was to hear it. He went on to explain where the Highlanders were located in Violaine in reference to La Bassée. And so on that fateful day, German commander Rommel led his tank force across a canal and across the fields where we stood.

"There are about three hundred of them, and this is perfect tank country: it's flat, there is no cover."

I looked up. He was correct. I could see for kilometres across the beautiful surface of the French countryside.

My grandfather's job was to transport messages and commands from the battalion base to the soldiers of the company who were forward, closer to the battle in La Bassée. That day, David informed me, my grandfather had done exactly that. But that was not all.

I could feel my pulse racing. It was odd to be standing in the mud in northern France with a film crew and a small academic with regulation leather patches on the elbows of his tweed jacket, being handed an antique tome that would reveal something so essential about a blood relative I'd never met. How did this happen in my life?

I started reading the book that David had given me: "'The forward Companies were supplied with ammunition and in one case with a Bren gun, by the work of 2928278 Lance Corporal T. Darling, who on his motorcycle, and laden with ammunition boxes and other necessities for the Companies in La Bassée, made repeated journeys from Violaine to La Bassée along the fire-swept road.'"

"For 'his gallantry and devoted conduct,'" I went on to read, "'Lance Corporal Darling was recommended for, and later awarded, the Military Medal.'"

I glanced up in awe.

The road behind us, David said, was most likely the same one that Tommy Darling had valiantly driven down. His bike, filled with boxes of live ammunition, was a prime target for German tanks. Nonetheless, Tommy Darling had bravely continued to support his brothers in war.

"Had a bullet hit one of those boxes of ammunition," David added with a smile, "he would have probably gone up like a Roman candle."

Then he handed me the official citation, which explained why Tommy Darling had received his medal.

I read aloud once more: "Lance Corporal Darling rode forward on a motorcycle with two Bren weapons and ammunition as reinforcement. He carried out this risky and tough mission under mortar and machine gun fire!" At this last bit of knowledge, my voice drifted upward in amazement.

"Whoa! It's like the Commando comics!" I joked, referring to the jingoistic World War II comic novels I grew up with. "Mein Gott!"

Gott im Himmel!"

I suddenly imagined Tommy Darling bursting through plumes of smoke from around the corner where the trees abutted the road, rounds of ammunition and guns strewn about him, tanks and snipers shooting at him as he sped by on his bike, a determined and heroic smile spreading across his twenty-four-year-old face. I had such a strong sense of sadness right then that I had never met this man. I had a startling realisation. My granddad was Steve McQueen!!

"He's extremely irresponsible!" I spoke aloud. I had no idea how reckless Tommy Darling would become.

"He's reckless," David acknowledged. "I think he's also driven by two things."

"What are they?" I asked.

And then came the final blow, when David showed me that Tommy's battalion, the men he had thought of as his family for seven years, were the ones he was risking his life for, and that day, as the Germans surrounded the forward post, he must have realised there was nothing else he could do to help them.

"And they're trapped in La Bassée," I murmured, as the whole horror of the situation hit me.

"They're either trapped, or they're dead," David stated plainly.

I realised my granddad and I had something in common. I, too, coveted what I had not had in my childhood—security, approbation, and my father's love—and have strived to recreate the family experience throughout my adulthood. He appeared to be always looking for one, yet his real family was hundreds of miles away, and his army family was physically dying all around him.

Despite his efforts and those of his fellow soldiers, German tanks swiftly pushed on their positions, dividing the unit in two. More than 75% of them were trapped at La Bassée, where they were slain, captured, or went missing. Tommy Darling was one of the handful who remained at the battalion headquarters in Violaine. They retreated and were eventually evacuated from Dunkirk. Only seventy-nine of the initial eight hundred Cameron Highlanders who went to France returned to Britain.

It was time to leave the field and begin our journey back to London. David went into greater detail on the retreat to Dunkirk, including the emotional and psychological toll it took on the troops involved. Something he said about my grandfather, in particular, resonated with me.

"He is probably wondering, 'Why me?'" Why did I get lucky?'"

I started to feel as if I was at the beginning of Tommy Darling's demise.

On the train return to London, I was continuously thinking about my grandfather. He was becoming real to me. My hallway wall featured a guy, my grandfather, rather than just a portrait. Someone who, if he had lived, would have made a significant impact on my life. Someone I think I would have loved and who, perhaps, reminded me of myself.

"He's so reckless," I'd commented just this morning. And I began to reflect on how frequently that word had been used to describe me. I have a little of the devil in me, you see. I'm the one that wants to do handstands at a party, take the shortcut down the dark alley, or leap into the roaring ocean after a few tequila shots. Now, for the first time in my life, I understood where it all originated from.

It felt eerie to recognize traits in myself in a dead man.

I am fortunate to have a spouse who is a nice counterbalance to my irresponsibility. Grant is sometimes the voice of reason, talking me out of doing something rash that, while entertaining, is really not a good idea. Other times, I poke him and tell him he's being overly careful. I wished my granddad had someone in his life like Grant. The boldness he demonstrated on that road in France was incredible, and he was rewarded with the highest honour, but it was all for naught: he couldn't rescue his comrades. I was concerned that Tommy Darling had a warped picture of what was worth risking his life for.

I also couldn't get David's comment about him out of my head.

"Why me?" he had assumed my grandfather would have thought.

As a young lad, I frequently questioned the same thing.

Why did my father slap me so hard? What did I do to make him angry?

I came to believe that I, and my flaws, were the source of all my life's problems: my father's fury, my parents' failing marriage, and my inability to do anything correctly. My father only noticed me once, when he struck me. Then and the preceding few moments were the only times I felt I had his entire attention. But even as a little boy, I recognized that associating something so horrific with my father's attention was unhealthy. So I began to feel terrible for thinking that way, and I became increasingly persuaded that it was my fault that he had attacked me in the first place. It was a simple spiral to see from the future, but to a young boy, it looked justifiable. My father despised me, therefore it's only logical that I despised myself.

However, my mother disagreed with him. She told me that I was special and adored. In fact, having two such competing messages, while puzzling, was ultimately rather healthy. My father said I was useless, but my mother said I was precious. They couldn't both be right, but they balanced each other out, and I began to form my own opinions, not only about myself, but about everything around me. I believe this was also beneficial training for my future work. I didn't truly trust what either of my parents said about me, and I've used the same attitude when dealing with criticism of my work. "If you believe the good ones, you have to believe the bad ones" is my favourite adage. My personal viewpoint is the most significant factor in both my profession and my life.

I looked at my watch. We still had a long way to go. I typically enjoy long train journeys, but not today. I began to wonder whether my connection with Tommy Darling was just a weak attempt to soften the blow of "losing" my father. It was definitely good to have something else to focus on. Every waking moment that I wasn't on camera was filled with questions about how I was going to navigate my future among my current family and my potential new brood of relations, assuming they even wanted to acknowledge me. I kept thinking about the half sibling my father told me about. What was he like? Will we ever meet and be friends? And how would my new father react to his new kid being a celebrity, a famous actor in need of the fatherly love he thought he had been denied? Did I actually want it from him?

None of this could be resolved right now. Not until the DNA tests were completed.

The kit had arrived the day before, and Tom had come up that afternoon to offer a swab of saliva. When I returned to London, I would repeat the process, and we would send it to the lab and wait. We'd been told the findings would be out in a few days, but that felt long away. However, I realised that it had only been a week since I had been on that stage at the Hôtel du Cap with an angry Patti Smith, and I laughed at how quickly life could whisk you along. I tried to remember how I felt back then, and who I was. So much had happened that I could scarcely recognize myself in the photos from that night as I scrolled through my phone.

When I went home, the DNA test box was on the dining table, ready for me, like a lie detector exam in a murder mystery movie. It terrified me when I saw it. This was it; it was real and definitive. I was taking a test to check if my father was telling the truth, and my mother had an affair with me as a result. It seemed so crazy. Everything did, however. My life, which was usually chaotic and quirky, appeared completely bizarre now. I was going through this moment as if I were imprisoned on one of those moving walkways that take you through an aquarium, with sharks and manta rays floating overhead and around you. I was in the midst of it all, powerless to stop it, and all I wanted to do was return home and remain.

What I was about to undertake would either put an end to everything or create a whole new set of obstacles. I'd know whether my father was talking the truth or not. I couldn't understand why dad would lie about this, but I also knew I'd never been able to completely trust my father in my life. Regardless, the most difficult and upsetting element of discovering the truth would be telling my mother. Telling her I understood the secret she had kept from me for 45 years would be catastrophic for both of us. I knew she would never hurt me, but I also knew she would feel guilty about her own deception. I kept telling myself that she had her reasons. And, as much as I wanted to know them, I also didn't want to see my mother in pain again.

What if that weren't true? Where did that leave me? What would my father do if I confronted him about his lie? What if it was not a lie, but rather a misunderstanding? How would he treat me if he discovered that the youngster he had abused was indeed his son?

It was all simply too much.

I took a swab of my saliva in a little test tube, placed it in the box next to Tom's, and sealed it. Tomorrow morning, it would be winging its way to some lab, while I would be winging my way to the Imperial War Museum to meet another scientist who would tell me the next chapter in my grandfather's wild voyage through life.

Rather alarmingly, given the fragile state of both my and Tommy Darling's psyches at this point in our parallel storylines, the Imperial War Museum is located in the Bethlem Royal Hospital, popularly known as Bedlam, London's once famed mad prison.

CHAPTER 9
WOUNDS THAT TIME FORGOT

When I was twenty-eight, I experienced what I now refer to as a nervous breakdown. I now realise that it had been coming for years—wobbly moments of irrationality and fear, which I had attributed to weariness or stress, can clearly be linked back to the road that led me to Nervy B.

I think of it as the box in my attic. Our parents' house was silent. Part of this was due to not wanting to risk our father's wrath, so not communicating at all was the safest alternative. However, we never mentioned what we were going through or how it affected us. When my father was not present, Mum, Tom, and I would occasionally warn each other about what might incite his rage, express anger about the consequences of one of his actions, or indirectly empathise with our plight, but we never addressed what was truly going on: that we were living with a tyrant, someone who, I believe, was mentally ill. As our silence deepened, so did our denial.

We all eventually managed to get away from him. Tom and I reached adulthood and moved away, Tom at twenty-one to marry and me two years later at seventeen to attend acting school in Glasgow. Mary Darling began her own independent life shortly after. We all put on a phoney act of being fine. Fine. Normal. Of course we were not. You can't go through years of persistent cruelty and fear and not talk about it. It really bites you in the arse.

Tom and I are 6 years apart in age. That doesn't seem like a big deal today, but when I was ten and he was sixteen, it was. And when I was fifteen and he was twenty-one and he fled, I was devastated, not because I was losing the brother with whom I had shared a bedroom for so many years, because we didn't have much in common and weren't particularly close at the time, but because I was being left alone and there was no longer any buffer between my father's rage and me.

Later, when we were older, we'd get drunk with pals and discuss our childhoods and parents. But Tom and I would do it in a lighthearted manner, marvelling at the impossible jobs our father would assign us and the times he became upset, never mentioning the violence or dread he instilled.

So the box in the attic remained there, accumulating dust and neglected. I guess we eventually forgot all about it. However, the thing about boxes full of denial and years of unresolved sorrow and hurt is that eventually. ..They erupt.

My box started to explode in 1993. I'd been married to my wife for seven years when we decided to try for a kid. Suddenly, the concept of being a parent and what that entails began to pervade my thoughts, and my own experiences with my father flooded my mind. But not clearly or accurately for a long time, for I had packed them so well that the gates took a long time to open and the trickle turned into a deluge.

At first, all I did was panic. I attributed it to the fact that my wife and I were moving into a large new house, as well as the financial obligations that this unexpected change placed on me. Then we had a problem with our next-door neighbour, and I suspected that was the source. The property had a large garden, which I dedicated myself to restoring, but many peaceful moments were disrupted when I was digging or chopping away at brambles and felt my wife observing me. I suddenly couldn't go on. I grew irritated and irritable. I realised that her casually peering out the kitchen window or standing at the top of the grass, sometimes even giving me a drink or coming over for a talk, gave me the impression that my father was examining me. As I weeded the seedbeds in the nursery or cleaned out the tractor shed, I remembered being watched, and my entire body, my existence, connected that stare with the unavoidable possibility of being hit. My wife knew my father, and we had visited him a few times over the years, but she had no idea the extent of his abuse or his influence over me. I described my discomfort, and she was really understanding. She stopped looking at me.

Then, about the same time, I started preparing to play Hamlet. It was scheduled to tour England, concluding in a month-long performance at London's Donmar Warehouse. It was the most exciting and hard event of my career so far. My wife was playing Ophelia, so she would accompany me every step of the way. As I went more into my job, I realised that Hamlet didn't want to be there. He wanted to be absent. He wished to be back at university with his friends. He is sickened by his mother's quick marriage, and he is devastated to be urged by his father's ghost—a faraway man with whom I felt he had little in common—to avenge his death. To make matters worse, his girlfriend is leaving him, and his pals are spying on him. I concluded that Hamlet could not possibly be mad. He was sinking into the same deep water as me. He was also in the early stages of a nervous breakdown.

Spending so much time thinking about the concepts of being a father and son, as well as attempting to decipher the gradual stream of memories and thoughts regarding my own silent childhood, made it difficult for me to interact with my castmates. Of course, I was exhausted—Hamlet is a massive undertaking—but I began to exploit my weariness, as well as the need for isolation to prepare for the performances, to mask what was a genuine incapacity to think of anything else. I pushed my friends and wife far away.

I started wondering what type of father I would be. I had seen and read enough about psychology to be concerned that I would simply become my father, and the more I allowed myself to recall what it was like, the more frightened I grew. What had he really done? He was just a little strict and quick to lose his anger, wasn't he? He hits me occasionally, but everyone's father does, don't they? He called me useless and worthless, but I've proved him wrong, haven't I? I was okay.

I was not like him. I was compassionate, I loved children, and I was not an angry person. I was a different man. I'd break the cycle.

Thinking back, I honestly don't remember any of the specifics of my father's abuse. Like my mother and Tom, I was still in denial. Fear and quiet will ensure this.

But, as the months passed, I became increasingly irritable, illogical, and incapable of communicating. Of course, the play was extremely emotional and taxing, but I sensed there was more to it. My wife and I were still trying for a kid, but I was secretly feeling increasingly relieved each month that we hadn't been successful. Ironically, my career was taking off in ways I never could have predicted. I started rehearsing to play the Emcee in Cabaret during the day and portray Hamlet at night. It was incredibly creative, but I felt more uncomfortable, anxious, and out of control than I had in my life. Here I was, the bright new London theatrical star, portraying Hamlet alongside his wife's Ophelia and set to have a family. I had everything going for me, but I felt powerless over anything.

I started to quit eating. I was already skinny from the play, but I started to enjoy eating as little as possible throughout the day. I became fascinated by how people noticed and worried about my weight. Of course, these are classic indications of an eating disorder: using food and your relationship to it as a smokescreen to avoid dealing with the true issue, while also believing that by starving your body, you are at least in control of something in your life.

I sobbed a lot throughout this period. Deciding what to wear in the morning irritated me. Of course, my wife was getting increasingly concerned and upset by my seeming inability to enjoy what should have been a happy occasion for both of us. When Cabaret began, I was introduced to a new group of folks who did not know me, which helped. But at home, I was a complete disaster. I remember one evening when a number of my very close friends came to see the show and then went out to supper. Naturally, they were taken aback by my weight. I sat at the end of the table, not talking to anyone and picking at a salad. I had forgotten how to be myself. Like Hamlet, I wished to be absent.

I couldn't recall many specifics about my youth. Instead, it felt like I was reliving the sorrow and sadness I had experienced as a youngster. I was doing this in an environment and at a period in my life that had nothing to do with the anguish I was experiencing or the conduct it caused. I didn't understand why I was so depressed. I just knew I needed to get away and spend some time alone to straighten myself out. I finally informed my wife that I didn't think I was ready to have children. Understandably, she was upset and outraged. I understood, but I couldn't explain why I'd changed my mind. I started to doubt if I really wanted to continue in my marriage. I was unfit to become a father. I wasn't fit to be a husband.

Cabaret stopped in the spring of 1994, and I was a zombie. I went to work, but if I didn't have an appointment, I spent most of the day in bed. I was deeply depressed. I knew my sadness was caused by my background and my father, but I didn't dare to explore deeper because I was worried I'd be unable to function. I needed to be fully away.

I was given a film in Ireland and jumped at the opportunity. Suddenly, I was away from London, from my failing marriage, and living in a historic abbey in the heart of County Kilkenny with yet another group of individuals who knew nothing about me. This allowed me to have time alone to think and reflect. That was a sentence I kept hearing and repeating to myself. Alan, you need to sort yourself out. By such and such a date, you should have resolved your issues.

The film was called Circle of Friends, and it provided a welcome break from my funk. But I didn't figure myself out. I thought a lot. I wrote a lot. I attempted to figure things out and determine what I wanted. I felt a lot of pressure to pretend I was improving, but I wasn't. The nicest part was that I got some rest, the urge to eat again, and the awareness that it would take more than a few months away from creating a film to get myself together.

When I returned to London, I moved out of my married house and into a small flat on Primrose Hill. I quit working. Now I'd truly sort myself out. I relocated to a horrible tiny place, which I believe was deliberate. I didn't want any distractions. I wanted it to be just me and my memories, and now the box in my attic has blown.

When I arrived at the Imperial War Museum the next morning, I met Professor Edgar Jones, a historian and military psychiatric expert. Of course, I thought that my grandfather had suffered psychological harm as a result of his horrible experience in France—how could he not?—but the rapidity with which I was dragged into discussing his mental health made me nervous. I was only getting to know him, chipping away at the picture in my hall and feeling actual flesh and blood (and such daring-do!), and now I was being forced to chisel away at his thinking. In the building that had formerly housed England's mentally ill.

"War changes people," was Edgar's first shot.

He had a pleasant expression. I had seen him chat to Elizabeth, the director, as the crew set up the lights, and I could tell he was uncomfortable with what he had to say. He was equally uncomfortable as I was. They were whispering as they flipped through the medical journals and military documents sprawled out in front of them. Of course, all of this was done to catch my shock on camera, which I was aware of. However, the need for secrecy and the prospect of shock created a real sense of foreboding. Another day, another bombshell, I told myself.

The night before, I had enjoyed spending time with Grant in my flat, and I felt my batteries had been replenished slightly. On Sunday, I'd return to Cape Town, South Africa, to continue working on a miniseries in which I was acting. Then there would be a month-long pause before I tackled the final piece of the Tommy Darling puzzle. I had told Grant the night before that having that amount of time would be beneficial, as the results of the DNA test, which we hoped to hear in a few days, would undoubtedly usher in a whole new level of family discovery and discussion. It would be good to focus on just one of my family riddles for a bit.

But, as much as I wanted an answer, I knew that the DNA results would cause massive emotional upheaval. If I wasn't my father's son, I'd have to confront my mother with the truth and figure out why she had kept it from me so long. Then I might begin the process of contacting my real father and new family. If it was not true, and my DNA exactly matched Tom's, I would have to approach my father and once again engage with his sick and nasty thinking, as well as inform my mother what he had accused her of. In any case, it appeared that my mother would be the most surprised of all of us, as she was central to all possibilities. I simply hoped that what I learned about her father would be more uplifting and positive than what I discovered about mine.

I let go of all thoughts about the coming month and focused on what Edgar was teaching me, which was simply that my grandfather could not have survived his military experience and trauma undamaged.

He went on to discuss how, during World War II, troops suffering from psychiatric issues were given rest, exercise, and occupational therapy, but few were ever treated with what we now call psychotherapy. The majority of patients went untreated. Even the terms "combat stress" and PTSD (post-traumatic stress disorder) are relatively new additions to the war lexicon, and were not in use in the 1940s. My grandfather was fearless in war, but he had to deal with the consequences of what he had seen later.

But worse was to come: if Tommy Darling had suffered mental damage as a result of his efforts in France, he would have little time to heal before being dispatched to India in 1942 with his fellow Cameron Highlanders. There, the Highlanders were challenged in completely different ways. They were schooled for jungle warfare.

The Japanese entered the war in 1941, following the bombing of Pearl Harbor, and immediately established a reputation for fearlessness and battling to the death. Edgar now drew out a map and showed me that by March 1944, Japanese forces had marched into Burma and were firmly focused on neighbouring India, the jewel in the British Empire's crown. They crossed the northeastern border and gathered their forces at the mountain town of Kohima, with the intention of pushing west to seize Delhi. I had a feeling this wouldn't end well.

The Cameron Highlanders were on the front lines of the battle of Kohima, tasked with pushing through Japanese forces positioned on a mountainside. The Highlanders faced mortar fire, grenades, and snipers. ...All with the understanding that the Japanese did not take prisoners. To be caught meant to be killed.

He hesitated for a while, and I took out Tommy Darling's Officer's Record of Service, a book given to me by my mother earlier this week. I had carefully examined it for any indications.

In the book, I discovered that my grandfather was admitted to a hospital on May 18, 1944, following the conflict. There were three letters next to the entry.

"What exactly does this mean, G.S.W.?" I asked.

"It's a general acronym for gunshot wound," Edgar added.

The entry also said "left hand, right knee," and "ankle," which Edgar assumed suggested Tommy Darling had been hit by shrapnel. His wounds were dirty.

My stomach lurched slightly. What a horrifying image.

The book Mum had given me also revealed that Tommy Darling was admitted to a hospital in DehraDun, northwest of Kohima, two weeks after being injured in the Battle of Kohima. Seven months later, in December 1944, he was sent to another hospital in Deolali, about a thousand miles distant, where he spent two months before returning to service.

Why had he been transferred so far in the middle of his recovery?

There was a break in the book between May 1944 and 1946. I knew the missing two years would hold the key to Tommy Darling's riddle.

"What does that mean?" I inquired instantly. Edgar glanced at me with intense eyes and said, "It's possible that these documents were purposefully destroyed. We can't be certain.

And so, at Edgar's prodding, I returned to the prior entry. Tommy had been discharged from DehraDun Hospital and transported to Deolali.

"And you may have heard the term 'doolally,' which comes from Deolali. We've been wondering if he goes to a psychiatric unit in the public hospital at Deolali."

Oh, poor Tommy Darling.

Doolally was a word I used frequently as a child. I still periodically shoot it off. If someone was a little foolish or nuts, they were doolally. I had no idea it was from an Indian hospital, and I certainly never expected it to be used to describe my grandfather.

Everything began to make sense.

I could feel Edgar's dilemma—his human reluctance to give me more bad news vs. his intellectual urge to finish the theory and tell me the remainder of the story.

"Two horrible battles, possibly one of the most horrifying encounters of World War II, followed by serious wounds. .."Edgar let out slowly."

So there it was. Tommy Darling, the fearless daredevil of war on two continents who had watched his fellow soldiers, nay, his family, perish in front of him, had slipped through the gaps of sanity and disappeared.

And this was not acknowledged or discussed throughout World War II. "That makes more sense as to why they'd destroy those medical records, doesn't it?" I suddenly realised."

"These records were systematically destroyed after the Second World War if someone had a major psychiatric admission, because of the stigma attached to mental illness."

I suddenly felt a surge of rage toward the military establishment, towards a country that sent its poor young men to war and allowed their brains to become jumbled, only to destroy any record of such damage, heaping shame back on the very young men who had given and lost so much in the first place. It's no surprise that such a stigma persists today.

CHAPTER 10
BOX

There was a chamber at the top of our Panmure mansion named the

"Big Room." It was where Tom and I completed our assignments and played games. In the centre of the room, there was a table where we played Ping-Pong. After Tom left to live with his wife, it became my hideout. I would think about my future while gazing out at the infinite rolling fields of the estate that dropped down to the North Sea. It was also where our deep freeze was, so my mother would make periodic journeys upstairs to get food or dump a Tupperware container of leftovers. However, that room was primarily my domain.

The Big Room symbolised so many things to me. It provided great comfort on evenings when I went there to hide from my father's fury, listening to Kate Bush CDs and plotting my eventual escape. I remember vividly receiving the prospectus for the Royal Scottish Academy of Music and Drama and getting my first sights of the place that would become my sanctuary. I worked hard on my education in that room, too, pushing myself to be more focused and earnest, with the idea that every minute of study signified an hour or a day of freedom in the not-too-distant future.

One night, my father pierced the asylum's walls. Twas the night before my music "O" Level examination. I was doing well in the subject, but like any industrious, concerned student, I spent the night before a huge final exam cramming and reviewing the previous year's notes to ensure I was fully prepared.

Around 7:30 p.m., my father pushed open the door to the Big Room and stood behind me. My workstation was in the window that overlooked the nursery and our field, which was currently devoid of sheep and hence had been mowed.

"The field's been mowed," my father muttered in that grim, inevitable tone, and I knew this wasn't going to go well.

I turned around and looked at him. Surely he wouldn't... especially tonight.

"I have my 'O' Level music tomorrow," I pleaded.

"Never mind that," he muttered, already turning toward the door and his bedroom, where he would change before leaving for the evening to drink at the local bar or entertain one of his girlfriends.

"Get down to that field and rake up that grass!"

And he was gone.

"I have to study!" I exclaimed after him. My increasing teenage manhood has caused me to put up a bit of a struggle, if not a protest.

"Get it done," he exclaimed. And I realised I had no choice. I would have to skip my last-minute studies and spend the evening raking a full field of grass. It was as if my father had read my mind and understood that I had come to see school as the first step toward liberation. My father could not have taken a more deliberate action. He wanted me to fail.

I did the raking, eventually having to do it by flashlight as the sun set. I knew the repercussions of that field not being cleared before I left for school the next morning were unthinkable. With blistering palms, I dashed for the bus while my father slowly examined me across the sawmill yard. I felt like I'd never get away.

That night, when I returned home, he inquired how my exam went. I knew I had done well, but I didn't want to tell him that. I didn't want him to ever believe he was justified. I never did. Instead, I got even more eager to succeed.

My father's air force uniform hung in one of the Big Room's cupboards: a blue, thick wool, scratchy pair of baggy trousers and a short jacket. There was also a long, grey raincoat, which he claimed he wore when he first returned to "Civvy Street" or the real world, as the young men in the UK forces referred to it. When I left home to attend college, I took these items from my father, as well as a blue sweater-vest knitted by my mother for him. I didn't ask if I could have them because I already knew the answer. So, I snatched them.

I'm still unsure why I did this. It was the early 1980s, and everyone wore baggy, retro outfits, but that wasn't the only reason. In some ways, I believe the garments came to symbolise my connection with my father. I needed a piece of him, something other than negative memories and agony. I needed him to understand that I, too, could take, even if it was only things, rather than innocence or childhood. They also meant that it was not over. It would take several years to resolve.

The army suit and grey raincoat were finally lost or given away over the years, but the knitted blue sweater-vest remained. It is located upstairs in a closet in my house. I haven't worn it in decades, but I glimpse it occasionally as I reach for items on the high shelf it rests on. I occasionally pull it down and sniff it, pretending I can still feel him, or Panmure, and that period of my life. I recently noticed I wore it in my first headshots as an actress. I guess I needed to remind myself that no matter where my destiny took me, I should never forget where I came from. That sweater is still a portal to another time and life, but it also contributes to my happiness now because it is a part of me.

We left the Imperial War Museum and headed to lunch right away. We ate at the National Film Theatre café, and I remembered all the times I'd eaten there while living and working in London. When I was deep in despair after finishing my run of Hamlet, I introduced the film of Richard Burton's Broadway rendition of Hamlet. That night, I learned that seeing another version of what you've just done is never a good thing. You either speak the lines along with whoever is playing your part and are transported back into a black hole of your own interpretation, missing what you are viewing totally; or, as I did that night, you become rather irritated by the seemingly obvious and numerous mistakes that you are witnessing! Mr. Burton's remark to the players, "Speak the speech, I pray you,... trippingly on the tongue!" reminded me of my time working at the Royal National Theatre next door, as well as late-night drunken walks along the Thames with a man who was the latest in a line of lovers I had engaged with to fix their anger.

Just like when I was a child coping with my father, I assumed it was my fault that my lovers were so angry. Of course, I now realise that thinking that way was dumb, irrational, and self-destructive, but it was still a difficult habit to break.

My reverie was interrupted by some surprising news. Elizabeth gave me an email from the Burma Star Association, a veterans' organisation that they had contacted. It informed me that they had located someone who remembers my grandfather.

"'David Murray is a veteran of the Battle of Kohima, where he fought with Thomas Darling,'" I read aloud from the email. "'He's happy to meet with you and tell you what he remembers about him.'"

I got sideswiped for the umpteenth time that week. I never expected that anyone alive would remember my grandfather. It had never occurred to me.

But there was, and that afternoon we left for Bristol to meet David, who was now eighty-nine. Not only did this individual know Tommy Darling, but he also fought beside him as his superior.

A few hours later, we arrived in a lovely gated neighbourhood overlooking the Bristol Sound. David was an energetic old man with a glint in his eye. He was wearing a navy blue Cameron Highlanders hoodie, and there were signs of his army days all throughout his flat. The walls were covered with photographs from his time in service as well as battalion reunions. He was clearly a soldier through and through. I wondered how he would react to the topics I wanted to ask him, particularly about my grandfather's mental health. But first, he had another surprise in store for me.

"He was called Big Tam! "He was tall for his time!" David remarked cheerfully.

"He was called Big Tam?" I repeated in amazement.

"Oh, certainly, Big Tam, Darling. Yes!"

His beautiful, eager, smiling face returned my gaze. He was definitely enjoying his reminiscences.

"He was looked up to as—" I started.

"I looked up to him," he added. "Oh, and everyone my age looked up to him." A man like that, who had fought in battle, had been decorated for bravery, and had the service. Certainly, someone respected him. Men like him taught us our occupations. "They were the backbone of the battalion at the time."

He halted and looked out the window at the fading sun.

"Nobody ever argued with Tom Darling," he said gently.

David told me of a man who was strong, tough, and never spoke back. Despite his imposing stature and experience, he was also a gentle man. David regaled me with anecdotes about my grandfather's humour, all while keeping the guys under his command aware that he was their commander. We then started talking about the Battle of

Kohima, which they had fought in together.

David's tone altered as he recalled the events of that terrible night, how the troops marched up that hill to meet the Japanese, single file and almost silent due to their expert training. Four hundred Highlanders made it up the hill, ready to strike.

I questioned where my grandfather was at the time, pushing at the edge of my seat to absorb every word.

"So, Tam was with the carrier patrol, and they were with the front soldiers. As dusk came, the Japanese guns opened fire on us, creating a real war scenario." Despite the inherent horror of the narrative, David was nearly smiling as he recalled it, clearly in his element and full of pride in what he had accomplished all those years ago.

"The Naga huts were flaming, the cannons were firing, the smaller arms were exploding, and my mortar was thudding away in the distance. That night, a rainstorm broke out, and about half past two a.m., there was a flash of lightning, a roar of thunder, and two companies of Japanese emerged from the ground, shrieking.

"It was the most strange sound I had ever heard in my life." Tenno Heika Banzai! "May the emperor live a thousand years."

That was terrifying. By the end, the Cameron Highlanders had lost one hundred and five of the four hundred soldiers who had silently climbed the hill. A quarter of the unit was killed, wounded, or just missing.

Tam must have been injured that night, according to David, because he did not see him again for quite some time.

"The next time I saw him was in the aid post," David recounted. "The rain had begun, we had lost many soldiers, and we had bitten off more than we could chew for a short time. "And everyone was a little... realistic about things."

He paused, and I realised the euphemism was a description of the terrible melancholy that had descended on the regiment.

"And he had been affected, Tam had been affected." The look in his eyes told me he was attempting to shelter me from the actual tragedy of how severely my grandfather had been damaged.

"Do you suppose he was under some kind of combat stress? I just sensed he had—"

Before I could continue, something in David's expression altered, and he lurched forward in his chair for a second before catching himself and leaning back.

"I just checked myself from contradicting you," he said, and I swear there was a tear in his eye. He took a time to swallow.

"Nobody had heard of combat stress . . . in those days, sixty-five years ago now . . ."

"Yes, a long time," I replied uncomfortably.

"It was a different generation, we were different men, this was a different country."

He gazed at me regretfully through his steel-rimmed glasses, no longer the proud soldier recalling his valiant acts.

"I never thought I had any combat stress. But when I first got married, my wife woke me up and asked, "What are you shouting for Sergeant Barrett for?" And he was my old platoon sergeant, whose name I often yelled.

He bit his lip and shifted his head to one side for a moment.

"My small daughter came up behind me as I was kneeling down doing something in the house and yelled, 'Boof!' And she stated when I turned around, she realised I could have murdered her.

I sat silently. There was no way this man could have known how much he had helped me that day. To say I was grateful, or even in awe, would be an understatement.

David gave me a serious look.

"He was a good guy. He was one of the people I respected. I respected your grandfather."

"Thank you," I replied, pushing back tears.

CHAPTER 11
IN THE WAKE OF SILENCE

I had two more weeks of filming in Cape Town before returning to

New York, Grant, and moving on with my life. Fortunately, I was working every day, and the little free time I had was spent seeing friends in town or having dinner with the miniseries' producers and cast.

I told a few individuals the story. It just blurted out over a drink, but it was too quick, odd, and unsuitable to fully express itself. When I returned to New York, I realised I'd have to begin the process of normalising this chapter of my life, treating it as something that had occurred to me rather than something I was currently experiencing.

I felt an empty, nagging aching inside, as if someone had died or I had been attacked. Of course, both statements were accurate. My father was no longer alive to me, but he had already left his mark on me before I slammed the door on him. Technically, I suppose he closed the door on Tom and me sixteen years ago, on that frigid November afternoon when he returned to our childhood home with tears in his eyes. If this hadn't happened, I would have probably never spoken to him again. I decided I was grateful for the opportunity to receive true closure. Surprisingly, after all these years and everything that had happened, it seemed like an amicable split. No ill feelings, just utter amazement. I wished him luck. I really did. And, for the first time in my life, I felt bad for him.

Over the next three weeks, I chatted with Tom and Mum frequently. We checked in with each other to see where the other was in the grieving process, for that is exactly what it was. My mother had dreamed about the outcome of my participation on Who Do You Think You Are? as giving her the answers about her father that she had always desired. Instead, my father had intervened, ruining her chance of pure happiness. Mary Darling had no idea that her husband had held such negative feelings about her for so long. In the several conversations that followed, I began to construct preliminary hypotheses about why and, more significantly, when he began to suspect that I was not his son.

Mum remembered the night in question, which occurred at the hotel dance in Dunkeld many years ago. But her version of events was very different. She had not moved to another room. They hadn't been discovered. She explained that the man in question, my alleged father, had a drinking problem and that he needed to talk about it that night. So, not only was my father misinformed about what had happened between them, but he had also misinterpreted my mother's act of kindness and concern as betrayal and deception. Of course, that made complete sense. I remembered how easy my father could spot the negative in any conversation.

As we went more into the past, I became increasingly aware of how thoroughly and frequently my father manipulated reality to fit the paranoia-filled world he lived in. I remembered several times in my childhood when his fury flared irrationally. He would suddenly turn against someone or something for reasons that were frequently incomprehensible, especially to a young child, and he would usually not express them. As soon as his mind was made up, mentioning the person or object risked inciting his fury. Whether we liked it or not, we all had to make that person or thing disappear.

However, there were no outbursts of wrath during my conception. My father's account of the incident at the hotel, in which he grabbed my mother and said, "Well, there's no point in staying here any longer," did not ring true with her. It was as shocking for her to hear it as it was for me.

I asked Mum if she remembered anything about his behaviour while she was pregnant with me that indicated his mistrust. She could not.

Indeed, my mother told me a really poignant story about my father dashing down the hill to fetch her fish and chips from the village to satisfy her pregnant cravings, as well as how pleased he was when I was brought home from the hospital. But with that account of his uncommon attentiveness came another piece of reality.

"A man like your father, Alan, a proud man but an angry man, would never have let me through the door if he thought I was carrying another man's child."

She was right, of course. Although it was easy to think the problem was never raised between them in the years that followed, as with so many dark secrets in our home, it made no sense that my father would not have confronted her when she discovered she was pregnant with me. His pride would not have permitted him to remain silent.

So it became evident that at some time in the future, who knows when, he had concluded it was true.

I am confident that my father did not fabricate this story in order to harm or derail my life, despite the fact that he was successful in both. It was too rich and complicated a deception for that to be real. Also, and this was both a discovery and a blow to my heart, I knew he didn't care enough about me to go to such efforts.

It became evident that this myth was created to benefit only one person: himself. My father had determined this was real to make himself feel better about how he was treating my mother and hurting me. Of course, the terrible, obvious issue in this argument is that he had also been a monster to Tom. It did not make sense. But, of course, it shouldn't and cannot. I was attempting to understand my father's sociopathic behaviour, which was based on a massive delusion. It wasn't a stretch to believe that he may have found his own justification to justify Tom's cruelty as well. But every night, when sleep began to soothe the rattling in my brain, I would return to the same thought: I couldn't believe I was related to him. Maybe I had wanted it to be true so badly, maybe that longing had penetrated into my mentality, but suddenly I couldn't accept that I was his son. And, while I most certainly was, and I had the documentation to prove it, I knew with every fibre of my being that there was nothing other than blood that connected him to me. And this is what kept me going. I may have been a robotic transsexual acting machine by day and a concerned and depressed dinner companion by night, but there was a light at the end of the tunnel: I was not my father's child.

I returned to New York and immediately began working. I was scheduled to perform in concert for a week at Feinstein's, Michael Feinstein's namesake cabaret room at the Regency Hotel on the Upper East Side. I had played there for a week earlier in the spring and received a terrific reaction. I knew my song choices were probably a little idiosyncratic and certainly politically challenging for the club's typical demographic, but I believe that if you're honest, true to yourself, and committed, and especially if you use humour as both a tool and a balm, people will respect you more than if they agree with everything you say. It's actually a pretty fantastic motto for life: go into the unknown with honesty, devotion, and openness, and you'll be OK.

I had only started performing in concerts like this the previous year. For years, I'd longed to do my own show. On the rare occasions that I sang a song at a gala or benefit as Alan Cumming rather than in character, I was struck by how different it felt. I wanted to investigate that feeling more deeply one day. However, singing as myself caused many terrors. As previously said, I had no character to hide behind. I was singing as myself. That felt like a huge and terrifying jump to take, which is why I rarely did it until recently. I had an additional concern about singing in general. I can sing. I've sung in a number of plays and films over the years, and many years ago, my friend Forbes Masson and I issued an album as our comedy alter egos Victor and Barry. But I'm not one of those vocalists. You know, the Broadway belters and gorgeous singers. Even worse, now that I've been on Broadway and won a Tony Award for Best Actor in a Musical, I feel like more and more people expect me to be one of those vocalists. They expected me to have that kind of professional tone. And I simply don't. I don't want to, but one of the difficulties with getting more and more well-known (and, in this instance, well-known for something you don't feel very confident about) is that you feel there is an increasing risk of disappointing people.

I believe I was also inhibited by the perception that performers enjoy nothing more than standing up in front of a large audience and giving a speech or singing. Both of these activities, particularly the later, would send me into fits of terror, and even huge rehearsals might cause terrible, nearly insurmountable anxieties. So you can understand why I was hesitant to repeat the event.

I'm not usually so enthusiastic about acting. Except on opening evenings, I'm typically really calm about it.

Of course, the more you do anything, the more at ease you feel and the less frightening it becomes. I felt that the best way to overcome my shyness and embrace my urge to sing was to accept my manager's offer to do a concert in Lincoln Center's American Songbook series in February 2009.

And I was correct. The more I practised, the more calm I grew and the better I got. The more relaxed and proficient I became, the more I did it. Nowadays, I come up on stage on a daily basis to sing a song or a duet with someone, and while I still get worried, it's the good sort of nerves, the necessary kind, that keep you on your toes and the adrenaline flowing.

That first night, however, at the Allen Room of Jazz at Lincoln Center, a stunning venue with massive glass windows overlooking Columbus Circle and Central Park, I felt anything but relaxed. My manager came into my dressing room to see how I was doing before the first show, and I told her I wanted to punch her.

Ninety minutes later, I was ecstatic. I have finished it! Despite my concern, I went ahead and did it. And I appreciated it, as did the audience, and most importantly, I felt a connection. The most genuine and true connection can only be felt when you allow the audience to see inside of you. I was hooked. The next visit was the Sydney Opera House for the Mardi Gras carnival, followed by performances at the Vaudeville Theatre in London's West End and the Geffen Playhouse in Los Angeles. Yes, I've always believed in starting small.

And now here I was, back at Feinstein's, singing a song I'd written about my disdain for plastic surgery to a room full of people, many of whom had obviously had plastic surgery; telling stories about what I thought was the essential American experience—being on an M&M's float in the Macy's Thanksgiving Day Parade; then singing a searing, biting diatribe against all that is American, written by my musical director, Lance Horne; then asking the audience to contribute

You understand the gist. It defined eclectic, and it was just what I needed. Each night, I walked out onto the small stage, and for ninety minutes, my mind and body were utterly disconnected from what I'd previously experienced. Our days were spent leisurely, resting and walking our dogs through Central Park. Grant and I had agreed to stay in a suite at the hotel that housed Feinstein's, as I would be leaving in a week to finish my turn on Who Do You Think You Are?. Going up and down each day in the New York heat was taxing. So, every night, after the show, I could just go back through the kitchens, up the service elevator, and return to my room, my spouse, and true comfort.

Grant and I would have drinks there every night with the people who had come to see the performance, and I would tell them stories about Tommy Darling and Alex Cumming, the two men who had taken up so much of my time. It felt great to talk. Everyone was impressed with what I had to say. Their questions were thought-provoking and occasionally provided new insight into what I had uncovered. But ultimately I felt solidarity, support, and love, which are three things I never got from my father and believe Tommy Darling could have done with a lot more.

When I arrived at Newark Airport on Sunday morning, I was informed that my flight to Beijing had been delayed, and I would miss my connection in Kuala Lumpur. I was meant to come on Monday afternoon, spend the evening and get a decent night's sleep, and then begin filming on Tuesday. Unfortunately, I would not arrive until Tuesday morning and would have to immediately begin filming as soon as I landed, which is never an ideal circumstance, especially when you're going to go on camera without grooming after travelling for a day and a half!

I called Elizabeth, the director, and she assuaged my fears by explaining that the first day of filming would be rather light, and all I'd be doing was looking over a few documents in the hotel. There was nothing else to do but enjoy the opulence of the Air China lounge. As a self-proclaimed airline lounge whore, I had no issue with that.

After a week of cabaret and confession, I found myself relaxing in this expensive no-man's land. I thought back to my grandfather and the outcome of his story, which I knew would be explosive. As eager as I was to uncover the mystery of how he died, I was equally concerned about what I may discover.

I began recording in a hotel room overlooking Kuala Lumpur's many beauties, which were drenched by a massive thunderstorm this morning. We could see black clouds careening towards us from our vantage point in the sky, as well as lightning shining over the dozens of glass towers below.

Elizabeth's guarantee that the first day of filming would be "light" encouraged me as I fought with jet lag and the crew set up. On a table in front of me, certain official-looking documents were facedown until the cameras started rolling.

It was good to see everyone again. I'd only known these individuals for a week before our month-long vacation, but it was a long week in terms of what we'd all been through together, and being back with them felt good. And suddenly, the next week and the unavoidable news of Tommy Darling's death seemed less intimidating.

That mood would not last long. As the cameras started rolling, I turned over the first document. It was Tommy Darling's death certificate.

It originated from Malaysia's National Archive. It read:

ORIGINAL DEATH CERTIFICATE, POLICE LIEUTENANT T. DARLING; CAUSE OF DEATH: G.S. WOUND IN HEAD.

G.S. sustained a gunshot wound to the head. I moved on to the autopsy report. ..ON JUNE 22, 1951 AT 8 A.M. I PERFORMED AN AUTOPSY ON THE BODY OF AN ADULT MALE EUROPEAN IDENTIFIED AS P.C. 10112 AS T. DARLING, POLICE LIEUTENANT, AGE 35. The cause of death was shock and haemorrhage from a gunshot wound to the head. There was a gunshot wound to the head about three inches behind and level with the right ear, and there was no skin charring. The occipital lobes of the brain were severely lacerated, and a very misshaped bullet was recovered from the left occipital lobe of the brain.

Brutal. I was totally unprepared for this. If today was "light," what would the rest of the week be like?!

One gunshot wound to the entry around three inches behind and level with the right ear.

This was just wrong. I was told that he perished in an accident while cleaning his rifle. However, you do not clean your rifle by aiming it toward the side of your head. Then another thought struck me.

You don't kill yourself in that way either. Has my granddad been murdered?

What was happening here?

As if on cue, a massive, loud clap of thunder erupted over the sky. I leapt from my seat.

The lack of charring on my grandfather's flesh could only mean he was shot at close range, and the bullet entering the back of his skull meant he was executed in a paramilitary fashion. Finding out the truth about Tommy Darling's death seemed menacing, rather than liberating, as I had anticipated.

I had received some information on Cha'ah, the village where Tommy had been stationed. Because of its location on the main route through Malaya, it had become a hotspot for terrorist activities, and my grandfather's security squad patrolled it around the clock. Tommy Darling, I suspected, had died brutally at the hands of Maoist terrorists, maybe during a raid on his police station. What a sad and lonely way and location to die, I imagined.

That night, I had a vivid dream about Tommy Darling and the horrors he must have endured in his dying moments. In my dream, he was blindfolded, on his knees, with his wrists tied behind his back, and a young, slender, terrified Malayan lad placed a gun to his head. Everyone was yelling and panicked, but Tommy Darling remained quiet, save for a single tear that trickled out from behind his blindfold and landed undetected on the forest floor.

CHAPTER 12
GRANDFATHER'S LEGACY

I awoke at 4:30 a.m., sweaty and disoriented. I couldn't go back to sleep. I didn't really want to. I got up and practised yoga, but it didn't help. I decided to go on a walk. The sun was just starting to peep over the horizon. This hotel's gardens were lush and airy, with pools at either end, and beyond the perimeter fence lay the jungle in all its primaeval, verdant abundance.

I imagined my granddad standing here, staring out at the natural bounty, the burst of nature.

This is the air he would have inhaled, I assumed.

It was beautiful. It was magical.

I imagined what his life must have been like in St. Albans, with the frost, loneliness, twitching net curtains, and cruel little hedges. It's no surprise that he returned here, where there was this and he was someone.

I swim in the pool. It felt great to be underwater. Under water, my jet lag had no effect. I was the only survivor in a postapocalyptic paradise.

As I laid down on a chair, wondering what the day might bring, a door to the main building behind me creaked open, revealing a small man carrying a large bundle of towels. I watched him struggle towards me, his face peeking out from under his load from time to time to ensure he was still on the correct track.

He arrived at his station and placed the towels in a basket before picking up one and approaching me with both hands and a small bow.

"You have jet lag," he replied, smiling.

"Yes," I responded. "How do you know?"

"Only jet lag folks swim at 5:30!" He answered.

I laughed.

"You'll have a lovely day," he murmured, beginning to back away.

"I hope so," I said gently, smiling.

"No need to hope," he murmured over his shoulder. "Many happy things will happen to you today."

And then he left, leaving me alone. I shuddered, wrapped myself in a towel, and returned to my room.

After breakfast, we drove to Chaah, where I was taken to an ancient colonial-style country clubhouse equipped with elephant hoof side tables and different stuffed animal heads hung on the walls. Outside, a pool glistened in the scorching heat. I wanted to jump in. I wanted to do something other than what I was going to do.

At the other end of the room was an elderly English military guy who, I was told, had worked with my grandfather in the Malayan police force. His name was Roy Samson, and the moment I saw him, I sensed approaching calamity. Elizabeth was purposefully keeping Roy away till the crew arrived and we were set up on a patio outside. Then I sat and listened to him tell me about shooting teenage Communist guerrillas during jungle patrols. Roy's enjoyment in recalling these things did not sit well with me, and I interrupted him eagerly for information concerning my grandfather.

Poor Roy, he had the aspect of a man who no longer had the opportunity to spout out frequently, and now that he did, he was doing it with loquaciousness and even joy.

"When we killed someone, they were hauled back to the police station and displayed for the public for two reasons. First and first, they needed to be discovered. Second, we wanted the local populace to see what happens to terrorists, in order to prevent others from joining them. Now here are a few photos of those decorations for the police station, if I may use the term, which became Tom's responsibility."

He arranged several photographs on the raffia drinks table between us. They showed the lifeless bodies of young Asian males stretched out on the ground, with the British officers and their guides immediately behind them, squatting in a semicircle and beaming happily for the camera as if these young men were antelope or some other large game catch they had just taken in sport. Roy was among them. I was really disgusted. I paused for a few moments. I wanted to get up and leave this man. I knew he was going to tell me something shocking about my grandfather's death. But the way he was carelessly tossing images of individuals he had slain in front of me made me wonder if he would be as cavalier and insensitive about Tommy Darling's death. My stomach had begun to churn. The jet lag was setting up again. I only wanted to leap into the pool that gleamed behind me.

I gritted my teeth and held up another photo. A young man's deformed body could be seen in the front, his eyes closed and his lips open. Tommy Darling, who had been brought to Doolally to recover from the mental trauma caused by jungle warfare, was now once again confronted with the worst that humanity could inflict: murder, humiliation, and hubris.

Roy told me that this picture was shot immediately outside the Cha'ah police station. These bodies were literally dumped at my grandfather's porch.

I slumped back in my chair, astonished, my thoughts racing.

I looked over to Elizabeth. She nodded. We had previously agreed that I should get some broad information from Roy about life in the area. When I thought I'd heard enough, I'd ask the question I most wanted answered.

I steeled myself.

I asked Roy to explain how my grandfather had died. I hoped the look on my face communicated to him that I needed him to take it easy.

"Remember, I wasn't present when Tom died, so I can only tell you what the story was at the time. And that was because he was playing Russian roulette.

He kept talking, but my world halted. My brow furrowed in confusion, and I jerked backwards in my chair, attempting to get as far away from Roy Swanson and his terrible news as possible, just like I had from my brother six weeks before on my roof deck in London.

What about Russian Roulette? Russian Roulette?!

I placed both palms on my forehead, as if to protect my mind from more damage from Roy's relentless barrage. Then I smiled. The smirk of a man who believes there is nothing worse that he has ever heard.

I became acutely aware of the camera that was within feet from my face. This was the deal, of course. I had finally solved the mystery of my grandfather's death, but now the world would see me sad, vulnerable, and honest. This was truly reality television. Roy kept chatting.

"I can tell you today that he had no known cause to purposely murder himself. And the conclusion I came to myself was that he either became irresponsible, ran out of luck, or both."

My eyes began to swell up with tears, but I didn't have time for that yet. I needed to stop Roy and clarify some things.

"Russian roulette?" Did people play that?" I succeeded.

"You feed a round into one chamber of a revolver—" Roy told me.

"Oh, I know what it is, I know," I said.

"And you put it on your head. I'm informed that someone who has done it before can determine by the feel of the gun whether the round is at the top, opposite the barrel, or at the bottom.

I nodded too long and too quickly, trying to stay cool.

"Was it customary to play Russian roulette here?" I asked.

"I believe it was for Tom. He had a reputation. The tale went that he had been playing it on a regular basis for a long time. My CO knew about it, he told us about it, and Tom's immediate superior would have known about it. And the only conclusion I can reach is that Tom was so respected as a police officer that they turned a blind eye to it."

My heart pounded. All I could think of was Mary Darling. I had to tell Mary Darling.

"I'm sorry to have to say that to you," he said.

I was surprised by his sudden politeness.

"Oh, do not worry. Do not worry. "I want to know," I said. I lied a little.

"And, as I say," he added, the brief shard of tenderness gone forever,

"I wasn't holding his hand at the time it happened."

I made no judgments on Tom Darling at all. I just tried to put everything together logically. The photographs, and Roy's statement about killing those folks, those ornaments, as he put it, I couldn't relate to that level of pandemonium. If that were your reality, I believe you'd have a very different perspective on the worth of life, including your own.

Mostly, I was heartbroken that my grandfather died alone, never knowing the emptiness he would leave behind. His life meant so little to him at the time that he probably never considered it.

We had a melancholy lunch in the club's main lounge. I sat at the opposite end of the table from Roy, eating in silence. I had taken Elizabeth to one side before lunch and asked her whether there would be any more surprises or terrible news later in the day.

"To be honest," my reply was, "I'm feeling really shaky and I don't know if I can deal with any more revelations."

She gave me a warm look. "There will be some revelations," she said.

I gasped and lowered my sight to the ground.

"But you will be quite happy with them. "Don't worry," she said.

It's difficult to talk about becoming famous. We live in a society that is obsessed with it, and it is regarded as the pinnacle of success in life.

I believe that social media platforms such as Facebook and Twitter are direct products of this preoccupation, as they help people who are not famous imagine what it's like to be famous. You share personal information and photographs with the public, and the more friends or followers you have, the less you know about who is watching or keeping track. It's fantastic to be popular, but there is a disadvantage.

Even so, most people, including individuals who are close to you and are aware of some of the more intrusive parts of celebrity, believe the wonderful aspects much outweigh the negative, and you should not complain but rather thank your fortunate stars if you are graced by the fame fairy. And to some extent, they are correct. Being famous is mostly beneficial. I have a truly fantastic life. I get to do a job I enjoy, I am paid well for it, and I am loved. Because I am famous, I have a voice and can influence change. And I receive lots of free stuff.

But

I'm constantly self-conscious. Every day, I spend a significant amount of time meeting or chatting with people I would prefer not interact with. I occasionally worry about my physical safety. Let's leave it there.

In preparation for filming Who Do You Think You Are? I reflected on how fortunate I was to have access to all of these resources and research teams, allowing me to offer my mother the gift of uncovering this family riddle. I often stated that this was the nicest thing that had ever occurred to me as a result of my fame, and I honestly meant it.

However, it no longer appeared to be the best option. Quite the opposite, in fact. I thought about the telegram Granny had received. This was true. Tommy Darling died in a shooting accident. I imagined the uproar I'd have to cause when I told my mother and uncles about the true nature of the accident, and I wished I hadn't embarked on this journey.

I felt quite selfish. This was my hunt, and now they would have to face the consequences.

But then I remembered the other quest I was on just now. I reflected on the lesson I had learned from my father's horrific chronicle and realised how vital it is to be open, how the truth is everything. And my Tommy Darling mission had been to discover the truth as well. It was only that the reality was so awful right now.

After lunch, I was driven into the actual settlement of Cha'ah, which is no longer a village but rather a lively little town with no traces of the terrible past its residents previously faced. I was going to see two local men who had met Tommy Darling. They were brothers, Datuk Rahman and Haji Ali, who were children when my grandfather visited. Their father was the head of the Malay community in Cha'ah at the time, and Tommy Darling was a close friend of his. As I walked up the walkway to their front door, I got a peculiar realisation that I was entering a home that Tommy Darling had visited several times.

I removed my shoes and left them on the porch before knocking on the screen door. Two small, smiling old guys approached me, hands outstretched. I immediately felt safe. We sat in the chill of their living room, and they shared their recollections of my grandfather.

"All the villagers at the time called him, in Malay, 'Tuan Darling.' 'Tuan' in Malay means 'Sir,'" Datuk Rahman smiled at me through his thick-lens glasses.

"Every morning at ten o'clock, he used to drive all the way around." His arm rose and sketched a circle above his head. "And then another in the afternoon, all around." He repeated the circle. "While driving around, he notices the children. Tuan Darling! Tuan Darling!'We all sobbed."

I could feel the men's concern for me, as well as a sense of optimism that they had something to offer me that would alleviate my anguish.

"I mean, the people really love him," Datuk Rahman said.

I wanted to know why the inhabitants of this town liked Tom Darling so much, especially considering he was only there for a brief time before dying.

"Well, he's the one who used to mix up all the gangs," Datuk Rahman admitted. "The community leaders, including my father, as well as a few others, such as the Chinese and Indian leaders, used to go out and have a nice time together. Do you know? They like drinking." Tuan Darling enjoyed a party and a small drink. I can sympathise.

Then I informed the brothers that I had learnt today how my grandfather had died. Their smiles vanished soon, and their heads lowered respectfully.

They told me how they found out. It'd been an extremely hot day. There was a river at the outskirts of the village, still within what had been the perimeter fence, and they had gone to swim when they noticed a man they recognized as my grandfather's police station assistant washing a bloody sheet in the water. They asked him what he was doing, and he explained that it was the sheet that had been placed around the head of their beloved Tuan Darling as he was hurried to the hospital in a hopeless bid to save his life.

I could tell that even after all these years, the image of that gory sheet continued to torment these sweet elderly men. We sat silently for a moment.

"Your father was very close with my grandfather," I said. "He must've been very upset."

"Yes," Haji Ali said regretfully.

"Yes," replied his brother. "That's why he himself put up the road name, the 'Darling.'"

I was incredulous. They named a street after my grandfather? I couldn't understand why a road sign moved me so much, but it did.

"Yes. "Walk, darling," Datuk Rahman said with a smile.

"Darling Walk," said his brother.

"Darling Walk?" I inquired again, as if I couldn't believe such a lovely event could have occurred given what I had heard today.

"The local leaders here respect him, very high respect," added Datuk Rahman.

"He'd done a good job."

I smiled at both men and thanked them. They had no idea how deeply that last sentence struck me. Throughout my childhood, as I toiled my way through the exhausting, insurmountable series of tasks assigned to me by my father, I imagined that the end of my work would not be the silent inspection followed by the inexorable spiral into anger and the force of his hand propelling me off balance. I dreamed that one day I would not be hit, and that as he walked away from me, I would hear my father say the following words:

"You did a good job."

I felt connected to Tommy Darling in ways that went beyond our shared ancestry. We both missed the same thing growing up: fatherly affection. For different reasons, of course, but it was still a shared experience. We both strove to replace that need in our adult lives with family and love, as everyone does, as well as thrills and, sometimes, recklessness. Fortunately, I have always recovered from my irresponsibility. Tommy Darling didn't. But I also sensed restlessness in his soul, a desire to challenge himself, which I have felt throughout my life. I worried if I didn't have this work that gives me such wonderful, visceral release, if I'd pursue those pleasures in terrible ways. I know I enjoy the surge of excitement that runs through my veins. I wonder how far I would go to experience it if I didn't do what I do.

We left the brothers' house and walked into town, where I discovered not only a Tommy Darling-named road, but also a park. The brothers joyfully showed me the "Darling Walk" sign, and we strolled along the small paved road around the "Darling Walk Recreational Park," which included a children's playground, trees, and people strolling pleasantly. It all appeared fine.

These additional insights served to mitigate this morning's devastating news. To be able to inform my mother that there had been a park and a road on the other side of the world bearing her father's name all these years would be a welcome relief from the shock of how he had died. It felt natural that Tommy Darling touched those around him right up until the end of his life. He was a reckless man, incomprehensible but fascinating.

None of us knew he'd gone to Buckingham Palace to earn his Military Medal, but he did. Until now, we had no idea he was so wonderfully memorialised, but he was. He had made an enormous effect on these people. He was clearly a highly charismatic individual.

After our small stroll, the brothers took me to the exact location where the shooting had occurred.

"This is the place," Datuk Rahman stated soberly.

"This is it," declared Haji Ali.

"The coffee shop is there," the first brother added, pointing across the street to a little establishment. "They took the beer, bring to this tent."

He drew an imaginary line around the perimeter of the tent that had been set up on the town square fifty-nine years earlier. I imagined Tommy Darling and his comrades finishing their patrol, getting a beer, and strolling across the street to the tent for some shade. Then ...what? I didn't want to imagine what happened next. Not here, not as I stood in the same position. I gazed around me. There was a small girl coming down the slide in the playground, and another climbing onto a swing.

It was wonderful to see the children playing in the location where something so dreadful had occurred.

"Your grandfather is a hero, you know. "We highly respect him," Datuk Rahman added, softly touching my arm with his palm.

I got into the car alone. The team had to stay behind, and I had a lengthy journey home. I appreciated having time to myself. I needed some time where no one spoke to me, and no one showed or told me anything significant or life-changing. I was really spent. Elizabeth had planned ahead of time and kept a bottle of wine in the car's backseat. It was exactly what I needed.

I said my goodbyes to the brothers, promising to come with my mother one day to see her this memorial to the man they so admired. I opened the bottle and toasted Darling Walk as it passed by in the dusk. And then my thoughts wandered to the man himself, the man who had lived his life with the volume turned all the way up. I was flooded with love and admiration for him.

CHAPTER 13
JOURNEY ACROSS GENERATIONS

The following day, I found myself in the Malaysian National Archives, a beautiful complex of buildings nestled on a hill above Kuala Lumpur, where I was promised I would discover written proof to back up my grandfather's death.

A gentle lady named Gowri ushered me into a huge library. She vanished to get the necessary files, leaving the group to set up in silence.

Today I felt oddly tranquil. I knew the worst had passed. I knew we'd be going to nearby Singapore the next day to visit Tommy Darling's cemetery, but today felt like a transition between yesterday's shock and tomorrow's finality.

Gowri returned, gently placing a heavy folder of documents in front of me. It was designated as L773. Lieutenant T. Darling.

The first document I examined was a police telegraph that described the actual events of June 22, 1951.

Darling and Police Lieutenant Macdonald returned to Cha'ah from patrol at 12 p.m., entered a coffee shop for refreshments, and were joined by an Assistant Resettlement Officer. Darling asked the Assistant Resettlement Officer for the loan of his .38 revolver, took 5 bullets from the chamber, leaving one, spun the chamber, held the revolver to his head, behind his ear, and pulled the trigger. You'll recognize this as an old game called Russian roulette. Striker hit the single round, which killed Darling instantly.

I let the little piece of paper drop between my fingers.

Next, I discovered some correspondence between the Malayan police department and my grandmother. My gut immediately constricted, and I felt a lump in my throat. I remembered her, the cheerful figure who had always encouraged me to be mischievous, daring, and true to myself. Now I wondered if she recognized part of her spouse in the small kid she had spoiled all those years before.

Dear Mrs. Darling, please accept our heartfelt condolences on behalf of all members of the Force on your husband's passing. Thomas was holding a pistol when he accidentally fired a shot, resulting in his immediate death.

The letter went on to detail his burial, including the number of ceremonial rounds fired and floral tributes. I kept looking at the paper and took a deep, strong breath.

Of course. They didn't inform my grandmother what actually happened. How could they?

I considered how sensitive it had been of them to keep the true horror from her and her children. Then I noticed the next letter on the paper trail.

It came from Granny.

I knew her handwriting from the birthday cards and notes she had sent me over the years. I had the last one she ever sent me hung on my bookcases, so I was quite familiar with her handwriting.

Dear Sir, in response to your request regarding how I would like to dispose of my husband's effects, I would appreciate it if they could be shipped home. ..My eyes welled up with tears, and my throat tightened at the notion of her sitting down to write this letter, which I was holding in my hands right now.

...as the children would appreciate anything belonging to dad as a keepsake, as would I, because we have nothing to remember him by.

My poor, dear Granny. The man she had loved but didn't work out with had died on the other side of the planet, and she had nothing substantial to make sense of.

I recalled how the story of Tommy Darling's death had been passed down to me. Clearly, the vagueness of the Malayan police force's answer had been slightly enhanced or inflated over time. I began to recall the few times it had been spoken and the variations I had heard. I also remembered how the entire affair was spoken in slightly hushed tones, partially to avoid upsetting Granny, but also, as I now recall, because there was a sense of injustice on the part of the authorities in the way Granny was treated.

Then I read a series of internal memos dealing with the issue of my grandfather's officer's pension, and eventually, after much tossing and frothing and a desultory mention of "the widow," I saw to my horror the ratification of the decision not to award my granny her rightful widow's pension, the pension that, despite their separation, Tommy Darling still desired for her.

The reason they withheld this lifeline from my family was that his death did not meet the criteria outlined in some portion of the Malayan police regulation book.

Out of nowhere came memories of my grandmother working so many jobs in the fields of the farms around where she and her four children lived, scraping by, abruptly plunged into poverty after the support her husband had always offered vanished overnight.

Granny sent a few more letters inquiring about the pension and when it would begin, as well as how she had to borrow money and accept a temporary loan from the state to pay her family's costs. The letters then stopped. She must've received the message. She recognized the pension would not be arriving, if not the cause.

Anger swelled up within me. Tommy Darling had always worked

hard for his country. He had risked his life numerous times; it was a miracle he hadn't been slain in battle. Now, the very military system he had supported and promoted, which had shaped him into the man he is, is punishing him and his family for the consequences of his experiences. For I had no doubt that Tommy Darling blew his brains out in that tent on that lovely morning over sixty years ago as a result of the trauma he had experienced on the battlefield. He was undetected and mistreated, yet the man was sick.

Still irritated, I moved on to more mail dated a year later, this time on letterhead from the police department in Elgin, a town near my grandmother's home in Scotland. Apparently, the commissioner of police in Malaya had asked a sergeant from the station to go and examine Granny, possibly because she had relocated and they could not contact her. He wrote:

I interviewed her there, and she said she is the widow of a Police Lieutenant who died in Malaya in 1951. Mrs. Darling stated that a box containing her late husband's belongings had been sitting at Liverpool docks for a year. ..I raised my palm to my brow, as if to contain the anguish that I knew was bursting to come out at what I had seen in the following section of the sentence.

. ..She is unable to pay the four pounds carriage charge.

Tears streamed down my face.

I sobbed for my grandmother, my mother, and every working-class woman who had made similar sacrifices and been denied adequate closure and emotional salve because they had slipped through the system, no, had been failed by the system, and lacked the wherewithal to do so.

I let out several sorrowful breaths before being able to continue.

"Oh, my poor little grandmother. "That is so tragic."

I lowered my head into my hands and cried for a while. Everything I'd gone through in the last six weeks, from that revelation on the roof in London to yesterday's shock, came to an emotional halt in that library. And for all the horrors of Tommy Darling's narrative and the resurfacing of the past caused by my father's unexpected return into my life, it was this detail, this brutally human detail of a measly four pounds, that struck me the most.

Life can be so damned gloomy, I realised.

Imagine how relieved I was to read the next letter, which stated that the Malayan police had sent a postal order to my grandmother to cover the cost of transporting the property. That was the minimum they could do.

I've been thinking a lot lately about how a man I'd never met putting a gun to his head in a town on the other side of the world over sixty years ago influenced my attitude about money, and, in fact, the way I live my life.

Of course, we all learn from our parents, just as they do from theirs. Perhaps more crucially, we get insight from our situations and sense of security, or lack thereof. Mary Darling was thirteen years old when her life was flipped upside down, plunging her and her siblings into impoverished circumstances. I guess she taught me that having money is never certain. It could disappear at any time. So I've grown up wanting to feel secure about money, but only by treating it as something to be appreciated, shared, and not given power. I suppose I could have taken the opposite path and became one of those people who define themselves by their fortune. But I honestly believe that I have taken the understanding that things can change in an instant and incorporated it into my life philosophy: neither money nor work define me. I like them because they allow me to do many things I enjoy, but if I didn't have them, I'm confident I'd be able to find something else to do, survive, and be happy.

Sometimes the toughest part about change is the shock of the shift itself, rather than the new circumstances. Perhaps because of Tommy Darling's genetics and legacy, I welcome change, never take anything for granted, and never forget how fortunate I have been and am.

Later that day, we all visited the Coliseum Café. This was an old colonial hangout where military officers coming from Kuala Lumpur to their stations elsewhere in the country would meet. Again, I was in a location where Tommy Darling would almost certainly have been. Nothing seems to have altered much at the tavern since his visit. The yellow peeling walls were adorned with photographs of military personnel in formal attire, as well as framed newspaper articles on different critical issues to the clients, such as "When Your Servant Has Malaria!"

I grabbed a beer and sat in the window, watching the world go by while the team set up, relishing the sense of proximity and imagining how he must have sat here sipping a drink and gazing out on this same street. My journey was nearly complete, but I knew it would be with me for a long time. I began to wonder how Tommy Darling would have fared today, if he were a soldier in Afghanistan or Iraq, and how his life would have changed. I remembered the article I'd read the night before, jet-lagged and concentrated on his narrative and how to best explain it to my mother. Although combat stress, sometimes known as post-traumatic stress disorder, is now recognized as a medical disease by the military, it continues to be stigmatised by all segments of society, and there is no proven cure. Unfortunately, the article went on to state that suicide is the greatest cause of mortality among American citizens. Today, the army's rates have doubled since 2004. Perhaps Tommy Darling would not have done so well today either.

But as I finished my beer, I resolved to do something when I got home: a fund-raiser, some sort of tribute in Tommy's name that would benefit a PTSD organisation, in the hopes that someone, somewhere, would get the care he never received.

"His death is not so shocking when you consider his life," I said as the crew was assembled.

Elizabeth inquired whether I felt I had learned anything about myself. I looked into space and thought for a time.

"Finding out about him and having to share that with my mother and family has kind of reaffirmed my opinion that it's really important to be honest and upfront, with no secrets. Because, you know, the truth can hurt, but not knowing can hurt far more.

I wasn't simply talking about Tommy Darling. The two portions of this story now felt inextricably linked, reflecting one other flawlessly. I lost my father but got a grandfather. One of them had never sought the truth and lived a falsehood; the other's truth was kept from us because society thought it inappropriate. Both produced contention and misery. But now, both have combined to reaffirm for me what I already knew to be the only truth: there is no shame in being open and honest.

It was shame that kept us from realising what a wonderful man Tommy Darling was. And it was shame that caused my father to treat me, Tom, and my mother the way he did.

All those years ago, laying in the woodland grass at Panmure, I immediately rejected shame. Now my predecessors had shown to me how correct I had been all along.

The next day, we flew from Kuala Lumpur to Singapore before driving to Kranji Cemetery, where Tommy Darling is buried. As we strolled through the big stone sentry gates that guarded the grounds, I remembered how delighted Mary Darling had sounded when I told her this was the end of my voyage, and I promised to walk through these gates with her again one day.

There is a white cross-shaped memorial in the centre with a tall tower reaching out from it, and my grandfather's final burial place is immediately past it and to the right as far as you can walk.

I felt unexpectedly happy. I hadn't lost someone; I'd found someone and was here to congratulate him. He was in a lovely position, beneath a large tree. I paid my respects, and it was all done.

I said my sad goodbyes to the staff at a restaurant before being driven to the airport to return home. I was going to miss them. We had been through a lot together, and I was grateful for their thoughtfulness in my time of need.

I flew from Singapore to Tokyo, had a little layover, and was once again able to engage in lounge worship. Even this swanky Air Nippon lounge couldn't lift me out of the numbness that had set in. It was now Saturday morning, around 8 a.m. My internal clock was all over the place. I was having a sake Bloody Mary (I am extremely adaptive!) and Skyping with my assistant, who was at my house in the Catskills, preparing for the invasion of visitors visiting for the Fourth of July holiday weekend. The time was 8 p.m. The night before. I was excited to see Grant and my pals, but I was also a little nervous. I felt like one of those soldiers who returned from the battlefield a changed man. My house has a camera that overlooks the meadow and rolling hills beyond. It's supposed to be one of those security cameras you point at your house, but I appreciate how it shows me what I look out at while I'm up there. If I miss my life in the Catskills, it's just a few clicks away. You'd be surprised at how beneficial and soothing a few seconds staring at it on a computer screen can be.

That Saturday morning, or Friday night, depending on your perspective, I was able to observe my helper and friend Lance bouncing on the trampoline I had in the meadow. It seemed surreal to think that I would be there with them the next day (or later in the day). I was about to go on one of those wild excursions in which I would arrive before I had left. It was a fantastic metaphor for how my life felt at the time: strange and out of control. Everything I had known as certain and true had been stripped away, shook up, and then reintroduced into my life, and I was expected to keep on anyway. I suppose I had no choice.

I knew all I needed to do was give it time, let it sink in, and then reassess to see how I had changed.

For the time being, I planned to have another sake Bloody Mary and a plate of edamame before boarding a plane and crying while watching Sandra Bullock movies.

CHAPTER 14
INHERITANCE OF TRUTH

*O*ne of my favourite games is titled "Two Truths and a Lie."

You say three facts about yourself, two of which are true and one of which is a falsehood, and the other players must determine which is the lie. You can imagine how satisfying it was to be able to add "I recently discovered my grandfather died in Malaysia while playing Russian roulette" to my list of truths! Or how about this: "My father recently told me I wasn't his son, but he was lying" ?!

All summer, I found myself recounting the story to almost everyone with whom I spent more than a few minutes. I couldn't stop thinking and talking about it. I recognized that, as with any traumatic event, it was critical to give it weight, accept the impact it must be having on me, and utilise the discussion as a means to cleanse my system. That way, I'd be able to establish some distance, and hence some objectivity. That's the general notion, at least.

It's similar to when you break up with someone and can't stop talking about them until you've gotten it off your chest. Though, of course, having known many individuals who suffered from Compulsive Break-up Talking condition, and regrettably, having suffered from it myself more than a few times, I realised the danger was that my Compulsive Family Bombshell Talking syndrome can rapidly and easily turn into Boring Old Fart Who Can't Seem to Move On syndrome.

Although I'm joking, there were some parallels between my experience and coping with an ex. Or, more precisely, dealing with two ex-partners. My father was now officially out of my life. I would never speak to him again. My grandfather was also gone, as abruptly and dramatically as he had appeared.

Both of them left numerous unanswered questions behind. Both were charismatic individuals with strong personalities who made a mark on me on all levels: emotionally, spiritually, and genetically. Because of their departure, I was a different guy, and talking about them and sharing the narrative of my mad summer was my attempt to realign myself and clear a route through the devastation they had left behind so I could move on.

I went back to treatment. One of the most unpleasant aspects of starting with a new therapist, as I've discovered over the years, is having to catch them up on a lifetime's worth of your stories. And this can be rather time-consuming! However, given the gravity of what I had just seen, it was a healthy and instructive exercise for me to revisit my infancy and early life and provide perspective. It took a long time, though.

After a few months, I told my therapist at the end of a session, "I don't know why I'm here."

"What do you mean?" she asked, her expression both interested and calm.

"Well, I know why I'm here, of course. I just had a massive fucking ridiculous amount of shit happen to me. But, aside from that, I have a feeling there's another reason I needed to come visit you, and I'm not sure what it is.

I looked at one of the numerous clocks in the room. My time was up. I began to assemble my belongings. After a minute, she said, "I believe you are coming here because you know your father is dying and want to make peace with him."

I felt like I had been slapped in the face. It was so obvious and so correct. This was exactly what I was doing.

"Yes," I replied softly. "I think you're right." I went home and cried my eyes out.

The date for my Who Do You Think You Are? The episode approaches. Because of the filming in New York, I wouldn't be able to see it on BBC with my mother as I had intended, but we were both provided a DVD. It sat in my backpack for several days before I mustered the confidence to watch it. It seemed like I was taking a gamble by opening up a wound that had only recently healed. It surely did not pull any punches. There I was learning that my grandparents had split up, that Tommy Darling's medical records had been erased due to the psychological harm he had sustained, and, of course, the gory and terrible facts of Russian roulette.

It felt weird to feel sad for oneself. The few months since, combined with a change in my physical appearance (my body hair had grown back in—I no longer resembled the pale, hairless man-child on the screen), had created a healthy distance between the me then and the me now, allowing me to empathise with and relive the experience.

There was also the thrill of seeing myself absolutely caught off surprise. Even in a show like this, where everyone is meant to be ignoring the cameras and the audience is a fly on the wall, there is always some knowledge that they are being videotaped. Several times during my incident, all of that was peeled away when I received facts that truly shocked me. I saw myself as I had never seen myself on screen before: absolutely raw, vulnerable, and honest. It was fascinating, but not really enjoyable.

I could tell Mum was concerned about the show being broadcast. It's easy to forget how uncomfortable being on television can be for individuals who aren't used to it, but having really intimate information about your parents broadcast publicly was something she'd never experienced before.

Mary Darling eventually decided she wanted to watch the performance alone, and she spent the rest of the evening answering her phone, which was ringing nonstop with people from all walks of life wanting to tell her about what they'd just seen.

For the next few months, she received numerous inquiries concerning Tommy Darling's story. Some she knew, while others were strangers who had met him or known my grandmother. I think it was beneficial for her. Much like I felt compelled to continue expressing my dual family story, she was able to express herself in this way and was also intrigued to learn more about the father she never knew. She has now met several members of her father's family and continues to investigate both sides of our family tree, armed with all of the preliminary research done for the show before they decided my grandfather's tale was the one to focus on. I gave her two enormous binders full of documents, and she had a field day with them.

I started looking at PTSD organisations with the intention of organising a charity screening of the program in honour of my grandfather. I discovered Give an Hour and decided to contact them. The premise of this group was that mental health specialists would provide free hourly increments of mental health services to returning veterans from Iraq and Afghanistan, and in exchange, those who got this free care would volunteer an hour of their time to do some type of community service.

I appreciated how it was so straightforward and got right to the heart of the issue, as well as how the veterans receiving care could also offer something back in return.

I hoped that in some tiny manner, I could help those people in need by ensuring that they received proper psychological care, which my grandfather never received. However, that was not the only reason. I didn't realise it at the time, but now I see that this occurrence was also a gesture to my father. The more I've talked about him and my background with friends and mental health specialists, the more I believe he, too, suffered from an undetected mental ailment. It's not only his aggressiveness, volatility, or mood swings; it's his complete lack of empathy, his apparent unwillingness to consider the sentiments of others. Of course, my interactions with him throughout the course of that summer just reinforced this. I was not speaking with a rational man during those phone talks. There was a disconnect and egotism that was at times astonishing, such as his assumption that I must have known I wasn't his kid all along. He asked, "Did you not notice we never bonded?" Worst of all, there was no apology or indication that he recognized what he had put me through when I finally told him the truth. All of these thoughts run through my head on a frequent basis, convincing me that he is insane.

I am not a psychologist (though I have spent a lot of time in their company!) and, while I have theorised about what my father's condition(s) might have been, I am tired of it all, tired of wondering. This much I know: the benefit screening I hosted at the Tribeca Grand Hotel on Sunday, November 7, 2010, was a tribute to both Tommy Darling and Alex Cumming.

"This past summer has been really difficult for me, and so tonight is in some ways a form of closure," I stated in my remark before the program aired.

I had no clue there would be so much closure.

The next day, I learned that my father had died the night before.

Every year, I go to Boston to record the introductions for Masterpiece Mystery, just to irritate Patti Smith. It's a wonderful annual outing. My helper and grooming friend Michael had met me on the train from New York the previous afternoon. That evening, we had supper with my old friend John Tiffany, who was on a sabbatical at Harvard and was residing in Boston at the time. John had directed me in The Bacchae at the National Theatre of Scotland. We would soon begin working on our next project together, Macbeth.

After much laughter and a frigid walk back to the hotel in the snow, we were up early the next day and at the WGBH studios to begin filming. I was sitting in the makeup chair, perusing my emails, when I noticed one from my brother.

Hi, Alan. I hope all is good.

Please see the enclosed document and respond to it.

That was unusual, I thought. Tom wasn't normally this mysterious. But then I opened the attachment, and I realised why. Our father had returned to our lives, this time from beyond death.

Tom received a letter from our father's solicitor.

My heart pounded as I read it. The title in bold was "Your Late Father's Estate."

The man presented himself as the person in charge of the estate's winding up and stated that he was writing about our "potential Legal Rights claim."

I attempted to talk, but the whirr of Michael's hair dryer filled my ears, and I wasn't sure what to say. I had no notion what this meant. On the one hand, I felt like I was a living embodiment of one of the plots of the Mystery episodes I was going to launch, and on the other, I couldn't believe my father could still wield such power. He was the epitome of those buried mines that occasionally erupt after a fight has finished, combining the sorrow of the past with the carnage of the present in a perfect storm.

As you are aware, your father left a Will in which neither you nor your brother Alan were granted any items.

I had never considered that my father would have left anything to us, though I had wondered if I would ever receive the letter he had mentioned, the one that was supposed to be the harbinger of my true heritage. In the ensuing months, I had often reflected on how fortunate I had been to have had the opportunity to speak with him and get to the bottom of everything while he was still living, rather than being presented with a letter after his death. I couldn't believe I'd never have had the opportunity to question him, challenge him, and, of course, tell him he was wrong.

Regardless of whether your late father left a will, you are entitled to a share of his inheritance under Scots law. This share is known as Legal Rights.

What?! Regardless of his will? Does Scotland have a statute that overturns a father's will?

Legal rights are calculated by dividing the net moveable estate (excluding any property such as houses or flats) in two. The Will transfers one-half of the share, and the second half is referred to as the legitim or bairns' part.

It was all becoming evident. "Bairns" is the Scottish word for children. Essentially, at some point in its history, my country decided to adopt legislation to prevent errant fathers from failing to provide for their children after their own deaths.

This portion is then split by the number of children. In your father's situation, it would be split between you and your brother Alan.

Over the next few days, my brother and I were thrown into yet another tailspin by my father's actions. We vacillated between thinking we should take the money—it was ours legally, after all—and thinking that by doing so, we were receiving blood money.

We actually felt strongly and intensely about it. It wasn't about the money, though that was a wonderful surprise; it was more about feeling obligated to someone we didn't respect, who had made it apparent he didn't respect or love us.

We were both riled up, and we knew our father would have liked to see us worrying over one of his edicts.

Eventually, I spoke with the solicitor.

"We haven't decided exactly what to do yet, but I wanted to ask you a couple of questions to clear a few things up," I told you.

"Fire away!" he responded.

"Did my father realise that this would be the result of his will? I mean, would he have known about this? I asked.

"Absolutely," the lawyer answered clearly. "He would have been told about the Legal Rights issue when he made his will."

"And so, even though he knew that we were entitled to half his financial estate, he still made a decision to not name us?" I was stunned, and I couldn't bear to think about where this talk was going.

"That is correct," the lawyer replied.

"So he decided to actively keep us out of his written will in order that we would have to make the decision to take the money that was legally due us?" I replied.

"That would appear to be the case," was the response.

I then addressed my father by a term I rarely use and don't approve of, but it was the only acceptable nickname for such a heavy, manipulative, and cowardly move.

So basically, my father intended my brother and me to be in the situation we were in right now. It was one more blow to our emotions, one more fuck with our heads.

I could see my father's face when he was given the consequences of making his will the way he did. I watched him thinking about Tom and myself being forced to question, struggle, and suffer as we interpreted his actions, and he enjoyed the possibility of us doing so.

That was it for me. After a brief conversation with Tom, I contacted the solicitor back and informed him that we were accepting the money. I was calling the old bastard's bluff.

I wanted him to finally give something nice in our lives. I wanted to spend the money on something fun, important, and positive for our family, and I knew precisely what that would be.

TWO YEARS LATER, Grant, Tom and his wife, Sonja, and Mary Darling made what I can only describe as a pilgrimage to Malaysia, retracing both my and Tommy Darling's footsteps.

We flew from London, and despite a seven-hour layover in Abu Dhabi, we arrived refreshed and lean, having slept like champions in our first-class pods and receiving massages in the lounges of both our ports of call. While seeing Mary Darling, I realised where my lounge addiction came from.

We had a driver, Khairy, who had worked on the Who Do You Think You Are? production, and were assisted by Alan D'Cruz, the show's fixer, as they are known in film circles.

The first night we met Alan for drinks at the Coliseum Café, I could see a glint in my mother's eyes as she sipped her drink and imagined herself in a place where her father had once been.

The next day, we visited the Malaysian archives and were guided to a private room by the charming Gowri. We read through the correspondence about Tommy Darling's death and the subsequent letters to Granny. Tom, Mum, and I were all amazed at the prospect of seeing Granny's handwriting in a small room in an archive on the other side of the world. We learned more about Tommy Darling's life there, and it was great to see my mother so involved with her father's legacy.

The next day, we travelled south to Chaah, and I was aware that some of the journey would be quite unpleasant for my mother. I shouldn't have worried.

As we turned the corner into the street where Datuk Rahman and Raji Ali resided, I was surprised to see how busy it was. Car after car was parked all around the home, and I noticed a marquee and masses of people waving at us. I understood that these two little old men had literally pulled out the bunting for the arrival of Tuan Darling's kid.

The entire town seems to have halted. The village's elders had come for a feast at the brothers' home, and Mary Darling was the guest of honour. If she hadn't comprehended her father's attraction and legacy before, she must now, surrounded by people who, for the most part, had never met him but felt his impact and charm in the fabric of their lives.

After lunch, we visited the town square, walked down Darling Walk, and sat in Darling Recreational Park. The brothers told Mary Darling the same information they had told me that morning in 1951. I could see her struggling to keep her cool. As intriguing and revelatory as all of this was, and as lovely and gorgeous as these men were, she remained the little girl who had finally figured out where her father was. They wanted to snap a picture of her in the exact spot where he had shot himself. I could see her steeling herself for it, not wanting to appear impolite, but I could also tell the toll it was taking simply imagining the horror.

"Are you okay, Mum?" I inquired.

"Yes," she replied, unconvincingly.

"You don't have to take the picture if you don't want to."

She gestured to me that she didn't, and I gently but firmly ended the situation.

At a market, I chastised my mother for constantly running away and made her swear to warn us if she was going to a vendor in another direction.

"I'm worried I'm going to lose you, Mum," I whispered, allowing it to linger in the air for a while before she nodded, and we both knew something had changed forever. It was as if Tommy Darling hung above us, reminding us of the fragility of life, the value of family, and the strength of love.

We eventually drove to Singapore, and after visiting his cemetery, I overheard my mother utter something that made my heart skip a beat. It gave me hope to hear that I had done a fantastic job organising this trip, but more significantly, that performing this TV show, and becoming famous, was all worthwhile.

I had stepped away from the burial and gone to stand under a nearby tree to capture video of everyone else departing. As I photographed Grant and Mary Darling, my mother remarked, "Well, they say dreams do come true...."

When we got back to New York, Grant made a remark.

"You know the best thing about this whole trip?" asked the young man.

"What?" I responded.

"Your father wasn't mentioned once!"

And it was true. We never mentioned him. Not because we wanted to exclude him from this experience, or because we were embarrassed that he was unintentionally paying for this incredible journey. No, none of that. We just didn't think about him. He wasn't really important to us. He no longer held any authority over us.

CHAPTER 15
REFLECTIONS IN THE COBWEBS

That was meant to be the end, you understand.

Under that tree, beneath a cloudless Singaporean sky, Mary Darling walks by me, stating her dream has come true, accompanied by the guy I love, and followed by my lovely brother and sister-in-law. That was meant to be the end of the book.

Then, eight months later, shortly after Christmas 2012, Jack, my mother's companion for twenty-five years, died of a protracted illness. Grant and I travelled to Scotland for the funeral.

The night before the funeral, Grant, Tom, and I stayed at Mary Darling's. At supper, I mentioned that on our way back from Forfar, where Jack's funeral was held, I'd like to visit Panmure Estate, have a drive around, and show Grant where I grew up.

I was aware that the estate had stopped running in the manner that I had come to expect. The fields and plantations were divided, the sawmill was shuttered, and the numerous workers' homes were sold to anyone who wanted them.

We came through the east gates, the late afternoon sun casting long shadows of leafless trees across our faces like strobes.

It was just gorgeous. I realised I had grown up in breathtaking scenery but had not noticed. I assume my thoughts were elsewhere.

We drove the same path that Tom and I had taken on our last visit with our father nineteen years ago.

We came to a stop at the bridge, and I got out of the car and raced along the top of the cliff, which is too leafy and sloping to be called a cliff. I arrived at the stone engagement seat, which some earl had made for his fiancée to sit on during their courting trips in the forest. Grant rushed behind me, attempting to catch up while clicking away with his camera.

I felt so liberated. Isn't it funny? I felt comfortable and joyful. This was not an emotion I had expected to have that day.

The drives, once clean and manicured, have become boisterous and overgrown.

I gasped several times as we drove down through the sawmill yard to the house, a route I dreaded twice a day at school.

Everything had been knocked down. The sawmill was only a pillaged skeleton, and the tractor shed was a concrete square with weeds growing through it.

I felt my father's absence. He embodied order, neatness, spit, and polish. This was completely dilapidated. He was gone. As a result, I felt free to view my childhood home as if it were a box of old photos found in a cupboard.

The house was empty, but locked, of course. It had reportedly just been purchased. A weekend home for a wealthy family, most certainly.

It still felt huge. I anticipated it to be less scary now, but it remained dismal and menacing.

We wandered around the neglected yard, looking into the windows. It was exactly how I remembered it. There was the sink, and the kitchen had been changed slightly but remained essentially the same: a kitchen in a large stone home in the Angus countryside.

I noticed the small room off the main room where I had played the piano.

We spent only a few evenings in the Good Room throughout the year.

As I turned the bend into the house driveway, I noticed my father's silhouette through the net curtain of the office window. My heart skipped a beat, and I paused.

Grant later informed me that in the woods, I would run and leap over stones and fallen trees, but as we got closer to the house, I became slower and more calculated. Of course, the woods represented freedom to me, as well as fresh air, imagination, and the ability to remain unseen. The house was dark and silent, as if expecting the worst.

My hand was on the doorknob to the shed. I opened it and walked in. More than thirty years ago, my unreasonable and enraged father had held me down and clipped my hair with sheep shears.

I took in every fracture in the stone floor, every nail hammered into the crumbling plaster of the walls, until my sight settled on what I understood was my reflection in the cobwebs in the window.

I smiled.

If my father had been alive, I believe he would be very proud of me right now.

I was dressed in a tailored black suit, a white shirt, a slim black tie, black brogues, and well-groomed hair. Even my glasses were spotless.

I believe my father would have approved of me. I believe I would have eventually passed his test.

But I had returned here dressed like this out of respect for Jack, not for my father.

It didn't really matter what he thought.

I thought I looked perfectly good.

The contents of this book may not be copied, reproduced or transmitted without the express written permission of the author or publisher. Under no circumstances will the publisher or author be responsible or liable for any damages, compensation or monetary loss arising from the information contained in this book, whether directly or indirectly. .

Disclaimer Notice:

Although the author and publisher have made every effort to ensure the accuracy and completeness of the content, they do not, however, make any representations or warranties as to the accuracy, completeness, or reliability of the content. , suitability or availability of the information, products, services or related graphics contained in the book for any purpose. Readers are solely responsible for their use of the information contained in this book

Every effort has been made to make this book possible. If any omission or error has occurred unintentionally, the author and publisher will be happy to acknowledge it in upcoming versions.

Copyright © 2024

All rights reserved.

Printed in Great Britain
by Amazon